URBAN INDIANS

URBAN INDIANS

The Strangers in Canada's Cities

Larry Krotz

Photographs by John Paskievich

Hurtig Publishers Ltd.
Edmonton

Hurtig Publishers Ltd.
10560 105 Street
Edmonton, Alberta
T5H 2W7

Canadian Cataloguing in Publication Data

Krotz, Larry, 1947–
    Urban Indians, the strangers in Canada's cities

ISBN 0-88830-191-X

    1. Indians of North America — Urban residence.
2. Indians of North America — Prairie Provinces.
I. Title.

E78.P7K76   305.8'97'0712   C80-091065-6

Printed and bound in Canada

To my daughter Sarah,
and to all children, both native and white.
The future is theirs.

Contents

Acknowledgements

The author gratefully acknowledges the financial assistance of the St. Stephen's–Broadway Foundation in Winnipeg, the Explorations Division of the Canada Council, and the Manitoba Arts Council whose generosity made the research for this book possible.

I also want to acknowledge other writers whose work and writings in this field have provided light; Edgar Dosman, Heather Robertson, Harold Cardinal, Hugh and Karmel McCullum, Hugh Brody. In working on this book I made use of the research of and occasionally quoted from the following studies: *The Explosive Years: Indian and Métis Issues in Saskatchewan to 2001* by Ken Svenson, Department of Indian Affairs, Regina, 1978; *Manitoba: The Secretary's Interim Report to the Inter-Governmental Relations Subcommittee of Cabinet and Indian Services Committee*, Clement Blakeslee, 1976; *Winnipeg's Core Area: An Assessment of Conditions Affecting Law Enforcement*, Axworthy and Christie, Institute of Urban Studies, University of Winnipeg, 1975; *Report of the Feasibility Study for Neeginan Manitoba*, Damas and Smith Ltd., Winnipeg, 1975; *Indians On Skid Row*, Hugh Brody, Northern Science Research Group, Department of Indian Affairs, 1971.

The book also contains passages from *Regina: The Queen City* by Earl G. Drake, and *Indians without Tipis* by Dr. Bruce Sealey and Verna Kirkness.

The manuscript was painstakingly typed by Debbie Whyte in Winnipeg. I am grateful for the skill and proficiency of photographer John Paskievich, the patience and help of the many people who selflessly and courageously opened their homes and lives to a reporter, and the support of Gail and many friends.

Larry Krotz
Winnipeg
June 1980

The Indian Problem

I am at a seminar for social workers and teachers in a large conference room in downtown Winnipeg. The long tables are arranged in a precise U; thirty-five chairs and ashtrays, an urn filled with coffee, the vague hum of an air conditioner. The participants begin to drift in; young to middle-aged social workers, counsellors, welfare workers, teachers. White. A few more women than men; dressed casually, all carrying assorted briefcases and attaché cases; ready, by force of habit, to write things down. There is an air of subdued joviality prepared, at a moment's notice, to switch to earnestness. Nice people. People who show up on time and take their jobs seriously. People who want to learn. Today we are going to learn about Indians.

The young woman named Marie has never been to one of these gatherings before. She is brought into the room by one of the senior social workers and is offered a chair near the head of the tables. She seats herself woodenly, a set, terrified smile on her face. The buzz of the group pauses for a moment to acknowledge, like a brief salute, this curious interloper. Then Marie is introduced. She has been invited to tell the assembly what it "really feels like to be an Indian." She starts to speak. She is barely audible.

"When I came to Winnipeg," she says, "I just put my kids on a bus and came. I had no money." The people in the room sit forward in their chairs. They need desperately to hear what Marie has to say.

Everyone has to go back out there onto the streets and into the schools and hospitals and houses and has to continue making a living by working with Marie and Marie's children and Marie's parents and Marie's friends. To know, finally, what Marie thinks and feels is somehow more than just a matter of idle curiosity.

"I went to the welfare," Marie continues, "and demanded that they give me some money. They did. Then they asked me to go back home. I said no; I'm staying here; this is where I live and you have to help me. The welfare man gave me tickets back to Saskatchewan. I said I wouldn't take them. He was really mad but I just sat there. I must have sat there for an hour. They never knew what I was thinking inside. They just looked at how I looked, what I was wearing, they saw I'd been drinking. But all the time I had all these things inside of me."

Marie speaks haltingly, painfully, with long silences. When she finishes, the people around the U-shaped table sit back, exhausted. We have heard essentially what we expected to hear, one more time. And we still don't know what to do.

This is a book about Indians, and about cities. It is a book about Marie and people like her. And it is a book about the non-Indian people who meet Marie daily on the street, in her home, in their offices.

Canada's native people are moving into the cities. A quarter of Canada's treaty Indians now live off the reserves. There were, in 1976, 282,762 treaty Indian people in Canada. More than seventy thousand of them were living off reserves. As well, many of the more than a million Métis and non-status people are joining their cousins in a dramatic migration to the cities. Twenty years ago an Indian person in Edmonton or Regina or Winnipeg was a rare sight. Today native people form the largest recently-arrived ethnic minority in most western and prairie cities — Calgary, Edmonton, Regina, Saskatoon, Prince Albert, Winnipeg, Thunder Bay, and Vancouver. Winnipeg in 1976 had a native population estimated at forty to sixty thousand out of a total population of 578,000. Edmonton, whose total population changes every day, hovering at around six hundred thousand, has a native population estimated at thirty to forty thousand people. Regina's native population is growing so rapidly that a Department of Indian Affairs estimate in 1979 projected 27,151 native people — seventeen per cent of the city population — by 1981. The researcher allowed that this was likely a conservative estimate.

What is happening in Canadian cities is not unusual. All over the world indigenous peasant peoples are moving to urban areas in massive numbers. Once there, they face cultural, economic, and social struggles as they cope with their new environments. And the cities are forced to cope with an onslaught of new people; people to be housed, fed, educated, and fitted into the economic, social, political, and cultural life.

It could be, it ought to be, a dynamic moment in the history of the world, a moment filled with all sorts of welcomed possibilities. But it is more often a disturbing, paralyzing time. We continue as two worlds, the Indians and the other city-people; we/they. We are frightened and suspicious of one another. We think of each other as problems. People from Vancouver regularly and innocently ask if "the Indian problem is as bad in Winnipeg as it is in Vancouver." The Indians arrive in the cities and run up against closed doors and blank or hostile faces. We study one another from a distance. No one understands.

The city-dwellers are curious and scientific about it all. They devour the literature that falls into their hands. They commission investigations into every aspect of the supposedly exotic lives of this group of citizens and, at brighter moments, trot out the Maries in their midst in order to put a human face on the story, to have a good look at some flesh and blood. And still the gulf is wide, still they are perplexed and confused and unhappy.

There is, perhaps, something poetically just about the influx of native people to urban areas. For two hundred years the Indian has been the mythic skeleton in the collective white European–North American closet. He was there first when the Europeans "discovered" North America. He always had to be dealt with, whether through exploitation of his labour and his services, or through battles of extermination, or through conversion, socialization, and management, while the Europeans engineered their path of "progress" across the continent. He would never go away. The Indians lurked both physically and symbolically at the periphery of North American life, at the edge of consciousness; like some constant reminder of sins and of the European's fundamental failure to come to terms with the environment of the New World. They could be killed, they could be converted, they could be herded onto reservations but they would never go away. For a century they haunted society from the distance of their reservations through stories of their hunger and their poverty. They would not change. They would not even become "white men" when society decided that that might be the last desperate out. Now they have the ill manners not only to haunt from the distance of the reservation, but to move to the cities and haunt from within. Perhaps the final justice.

This book is written from the most elemental rationale a reporter ever has; a story must be told because it is there. And this story, I feel, is one of the most important stories of this decade in the tides that create Canadian life. Few stories and few human movements so confront our history; so confront our private fears and stereotypes; so confront our myths; and so leave us confused and paralyzed. Few events so allow for the best or the worst instincts in our society to emerge. Few stories are so tailor-made to characterize Canada.

The three cities that are written about most in this book — Edmonton, Regina, and Winnipeg — were taken arbitrarily. I could have written as easily about three other cities. These three are, nonetheless, sufficiently similar yet sufficiently different to provide important checks and contrasts. Similarly the people who talk about their lives or who are otherwise written about in the book were selected randomly, as I met them and as they were willing to share with a reporter. I would like to say that they represent a cross-section of native people in western Canadian cities. Perhaps they do; perhaps they represent only themselves. Their experiences, nonetheless, are authentic.

The photographs were taken for the book, but they were not taken to illustrate the book. They represent John Paskievich's impressions and are the result of his interactions with his subjects. They must be seen as a separate documentation. What I write and what Paskievich photographs are, I trust, in harmony, but they are not dependent on each other.

A Reserve
God's Lake Narrows, Manitoba

The same plane that brings in Mary Watt and her new twin daughters, swaddled in pink and blinking, red-faced, at the world, will take out for embalming the body of old Joe Nazzie, who drowned the day before. It costs $104 for a round trip between God's Lake Narrows and Winnipeg. There are three planes a day; little eight-seater Beechcrafts that make the three hundred miles northeast from the city over the southern part of Lake Winnipeg and then over the endless quiltwork of bush and muskeg in a little over two hours, if the wind is favourable. Sometimes there are more planes. The Mounties come in on a special plane. So do medical people and Indian Affairs officials. Sometimes tourists, well-off Americans who come to one of the three lodges in the area will charter in and that will be another plane.

Jet-age transportation is no stranger to the people of God's Narrows. Nor is Winnipeg. Even from this community that might be considered remote by any reasoned definition, Winnipeg is almost as much a focus of life as is the reserve or the Hudson's Bay store or the river. Expectant mothers are flown to Winnipeg a week ahead of time to ensure that there will be no surprises, even though the nurses at the nursing station are both competent midwives. And the bodies of the dead are flown out for embalming, or, should the circumstances of death warrant it, for an autopsy. Bodies are gone a week before they are returned for the customary wake and burial.

Between birth and death, the trip out is made so frequently by some people that theirs could almost be called a commuter lifestyle. Meetings for band officials take place in Winnipeg. A child who proceeds beyond grade twelve in school goes to Winnipeg for the additional training. It is only recently that children didn't have to go out for anything after grade nine. Many residents of God's Narrows now in their twenties or early thirties can tell stories of two years or three years living in Winnipeg in a church-run residence or boarding in a private home while they attended high school or a year or two of trade school. People go to Winnipeg for economic reasons; the fur markets, if one chooses to by-pass the Bay trader, are in Winnipeg. Or people go for social reasons. Arthur Okimow, the chief's son, describes the hotel he regularly stays in. Another young man says that he goes to Winnipeg for a couple of days whenever it gets a bit boring at God's Lake, perhaps once a month. A young couple go to Winnipeg to visit their parents who moved there when they got too old to cut the wood and haul the water they needed to keep themselves going at God's Lake Narrows. Now they live in the city on two pension cheques and get their heat by flipping a switch and their water by turning a tap, and their children come to visit and stay for as long as a month. Every May there is a Shriners' circus in Winnipeg at about the same time that income-tax refunds arrive. An airline official tells me that the two hundred dollars most people get as a child tax credit is just enough to buy a return plane ticket, a pass to the circus, a couple of meals, and a night in an inexpensive hotel. For a week the planes are full and a reservation can't be had.

Through the combined modern marvels of cash, credit, and air travel the Indian societies of places like God's Lake Narrows have returned to being migratory societies. But the movement is not as it was, following the furs and making trips to the trading posts, or moving annually from the settled community out to the summer fishing camps. It is between the reserve, perched on the narrows of a lake up in the northeast corner of Manitoba, and the city, the huge metropolis sitting on the plain three hundred air miles to the south. Winnipeg is very close to the psyche of God's Lake Narrows. In the band office are posters advertising the Friendship Centre in Winnipeg and also western hour at the Epic Theatre on Main Street.

God's Lake Narrows is a northern Indian reservation in the classic style. Twelve hundred people live there, their houses strung out along a height of land on the south side of the narrows of the lake. This is the reserve. Most are treaty Indians, Cree, with a handful of Métis or mixed bloods, the offspring of white traders of years ago, living at the edge of the reserve. Across the narrows in the government and Hudson's Bay Company compounds live the few white permanent officials; the nurses, the Bayman, the conservation officer from the Department of Natural Resources, the airport manager. Also on the white side of the narrows is the fishing lodge. The lodge manages to keep busy all year because it accommodates not only fishermen and hunters, but also functions as the hotel for whoever is passing through; Indian Affairs officials, telephone repairmen, construction workers, court parties. At the east end, on reserve land, is the school, a large new orange and brown modern structure complete with gymnasium and workshops. Behind the school is a motel-like building that is the residence for the teachers.

There are no fences on the reserve. In fact there are no such things as yards. When walking around the reserve one takes the road only part of the time. Other times, one takes pathways that form the most direct route to any particular place. These pathways often cut to within inches of someone's front door, go between houses and their privies, or under people's clothes lines. In contrast, everything in the white part of the community is fenced. There are white pole fences all around the property of the Hudson's Bay store and the nursing station. The teachers' housing at the school is fenced in part with a white picket fence and in part with a formidable looking chain-link fence.

The people at God's Lake Narrows are Woodland Cree. For centuries their ancestors wandered through this country fishing, hunting, and gathering. In 1909, when the Hudson's Bay Company placed a post at the narrows, the site became a focal point for the people. Now three hundred families live on the reserve. Life seems idyllic: the lake and the deep, black, cold water beautiful in a Laurentian kind of way against the backdrop of granite outcrops and spruce and pine forest. The lakes wind on forever, one leading into another in a network that stretches into the infinite distance. They abound in trout, jackfish, and pickerel. The pickerel are so good and so plentiful that fishermen throw the jackfish away. The forest cover is not thick, actually parkland, so it is a good country for moose. Fur animals abound. But life is also hard. Water for the households comes from the narrows. In winter the women or the children edge their way sideways down the steep rock slope to the ice and walk out across it to a hole that has been chopped in its three-foot thickness, and they dip for their water. Then they carry it back up the slippery path and along to their homes, perhaps a quarter of a mile away. All their water is drawn in this fashion. When I visited God's Lake Narrows the band was building a water line from one end of the reserve to the other with a huge pump at the intake at the shore. When it is finished, there will be taps every hundred yards up through the community and people won't have to go

as far for their water, at least they won't have to go down the steep path to the shore. While the line was being built, a big ditch snaked like an open sore through the community. But the people were excited that their water was going to be a little more convenient. The whites' side of the narrows has had running water and septic facilities for years.

As is the case on many reserves, the life of God's Lake Narrows is characterized by three things: a growing preoccupation with the life of the broader world, represented here by Winnipeg; a chafing and a sullen dissatisfaction with the government service bureaucracies that pervade everyone's life; and a thin and precarious local economy.

The first commercial fishing at God's Lake Narrows was done in 1934. Now there is some commercial fishing done in winter through the ice, but none in summer because it would take business away from the three lodges which cater to American tourists. The lodges also need the Indian men to work as guides. They look after the gear, take the fishermen out, cook their lunch in the bush, and clean any fish they might catch. For this they have been getting $35 a day. The band council is talking about getting it raised to $50. Some men still trap; muskrat and beaver are the staple pelts with a smattering of other more exotic furs; lynx, wolf, marten, and so on. Another employer, the biggest, is the band itself. It hires men to drive trucks or the band tractor or the school bus. It hires people to work on the water system that is being installed or to clean up garbage or to build houses or to freight supplies across from the airport to the band store. The local government is the biggest employer with a hundred bits of sporadic and part-time work available. It pays to be in good with the chief or a powerful councillor if you want any of this work.

The Economic Development Officer who works for the Department of Indian Affairs flies in regularly from Winnipeg. He is in charge of three reserves in this part of the province. He says that fewer than ten men fish for a living at God's Lake Narrows. Fifty people are employed by the band council doing various jobs, and forty to fifty men guide for the lodges during June and July. This is out of a reserve of twelve hundred people. More than fifty per cent of the people subsist on welfare.

The Economic Development Officer complains about the houses on the reserve. They are standard Indian Affairs plywood and two-by-four houses that cost around five hundred dollars to heat for a winter and tend to fall apart in five years. He says that you can't get financing for alternate construction styles like stack-wall or log because those aren't styles approved by Central Mortgage and Housing. He also says that log or stack-wall would be expensive to build because a lot of labour is required and labour is expensive. But with fifty per cent of the people on welfare, it would seem that labour is all God's Lake Narrows has!

People complain about the houses Indian Affairs builds. People complain about many things. An elderly fisherman stops me and asks if I am a lawyer. He says that he has been trying for two years to get eyeglasses. The enterprise has involved a trip to Winnipeg and two visits to Thompson. The optometrists pass him to federal medical services people who in turn pass him to the chief of his band who passes him back to medical services. Time goes by and he continues to see double. A little bit of service if sought from up here requires an enormous amount of red-tape cutting.

People complain about the nurses. They say that they are inaccessible. The nursing station is on the white side of the narrows and the nurses don't make house-calls. The nurses say that they do make check-up calls to old people and young mothers but no house-calls for emergencies. They say they resent being wakened at two in the morning because somebody has been hurt in a drunken fight. The nurses' policy is "no ambulance service; make them come to us." So if someone wants to see a nurse, it involves getting in a boat to cross the narrows in summer, or onto a Ski-doo in winter. And if they require attention that is greater than a Band-Aid or an Aspirin chances are they will be shipped out to Winnipeg. A doctor comes to God's Lake Narrows two days each week from Winnipeg, but all serious injuries and illnesses go out for attention.

The principal at the school says that he would like to see Cree used as the language of instruction up to grade four. For the Indian people this would be a tremendous victory, one they have been seeking for decades. In the old days, in the residential schools, little children were punished for speaking their Indian language. Later, though the beatings stopped, children still suffered the agonies of being labelled as retarded or slow, not because they were either of these things, but because they were struggling to learn facts and concepts that were foreign to them and they were trying to learn these things in a strange language. So the moves to use Indian languages in the lower grades of the schools should be met with great cheering. Except for one thing. With the irony that pervades many of the things that happen to Indian people, this move to change the language policies of the schools comes at a time when such a policy is likely to be most redundant. Why? Television.

Television came to God's Lake Narrows in the autumn of 1978. There is a tall transmitter at the edge of the community that brings in the CBC signal. Every house in the community has a television. Some houses have two. Overnight God's Lake Narrows has changed. The kids learn English now not because the teacher in the school threatens to whip them if they speak Cree, but because that's the language the Cookie Monster talks on *Sesame Street* and they see him every morning from the time they are able to focus their eyes in the crib. Given television, Indian language will become an anachronism and the teaching of it in the school will not serve as rectification of an historical wrong. It will, instead, be like teaching a folklore; it will be redundant.

Television has other influences. A six-year study on the effects of television in northern native communities has been undertaken by doctors Jack Steinbring and Gary Granzburg of the University of Winnipeg anthropology department. Not the least of the influences of television is that through it, for better or worse, formerly remote places like God's Lake Narrows and several dozen others like it stretching across the north of Canada, become intricately laced in with the rest of the world. Television is the great leveller; the great democratizer. Studies show that the average North American household has the set on for six hours each day. I suspect that, particularly until its novelty wears off, the average set in God's Lake Narrows is on for much longer each day, if simply because there is little else to do. The tube, the box in the front room of each little house, has brought in the world, or at least the Hollywood concept of the world, and has made God's Lake Narrows a part of that world.

When I visited God's Lake Narrows the Stanley Cup hockey play-offs were on. After eight o'clock at night not a soul was to be seen out-of-doors. Every set in the community was turned on. The band office wall had elaborate betting pools pinned up on it. The loyalties of the community were split between the Rangers and the Canadiens. Little kids pretended they were Ken Dryden when their brothers slapped a rubber ball at their shins. Never before had people taken this interest in the Stanley Cup. Before, Montreal and New York were vague references that meant little. Hardly anyone had even seen a real hockey game save for the shinny they taught the kids to play at the school. Hockey became, through the medium of television, a big thing. The community built a rink so that the men could play hockey. The councillors now could pretend they too were Ken Dryden. The same thing occurred with politics. By seeing Joe Clark and Pierre Trudeau and Ed Broadbent on television at night, the people at last could understand why the rest of the world could get excited about an election. They too got excited. Some of the men started wearing political buttons. All because of television. Now when the children start school they will be scratching their heads when the teacher tries to teach them in Cree. Now when they go to Winnipeg it won't seem so strange. They will have seen it all on television.

Bev Desnomie, Regina

"I'm one of the lucky ones," says Bev. She is twenty-two with two kids and carrying a third. We sit in the cluttered office at the Regina Native Women's Association, a catch-all of programs, assistance, housing, and advocacy for Indian women in that city. Bev is working there, training to be an administrator. What she means when she says she is lucky is that she has two of life's aces in her hand; she has a job, and she has a man back home who waits for her. Home for Bev is the Peepeekisis reserve a hundred kilometers northeast of Regina near the little farm town of Balcarres. She has been in Regina since October 1977.

Pretty and plump, with long black hair, luminescent skin, and wide eyes framed by wire glasses, she talks simply and honestly with only an occasional hesitation.

All my friends are from Peepeekisis; if they move into Regina, I will go to visit them and they will visit me. But I really don't have that much contact because I spend all my weekends out on the reserve with my family. There's four reserves close together where I come from and we just move from one to the next, visiting people. Regina is just a place to work. There's lots of commuting. Maybe everybody doesn't go back to their own reserve, but, especially in the summer, everybody leaves the city on weekends. All summer long there are celebrations on different reserves around the province and people go to these. I have my parents' car so I go out every Friday night and come back on Sunday night.

Denby, that's who I stay with, works in the Department of Highways in Balcarres. He's very fortunate to have that job. When you live on a reserve it's very rare that you will get a job off the reserve that is close to the reserve. Balcarres is only about eight miles from the reserve. Denby's interested in the rodeo so on weekends sometimes he'll go to the rodeos and I'll go stay at my parents' place. Sometimes I used to go to the rodeos but since I'm going to have my baby I don't want to go anywhere.

When I first left the reserve I worked for five months at Lebreque residential school, just a temporary job. They hired me to help them with their accounting because I had some secretarial training; I had worked in the band office for a year.

Then my second boy Anthony was born. I had him in Saskatoon, I went and stayed at my aunt's place in Saskatoon. I babysat for her until I had the baby. Then I went back to the reserve for a couple of months. But it was really ugly on the reserve. My mother, my sister Vera, my four little brothers, my Dad, my sister Sandra and her boyfriend John, they were working out but they were staying at mom's in the evenings, and me and Denby and the two boys. That's thirteen people all staying in one house. We were just getting in each others' way. Also it was getting close to winter, it was October, so nobody wanted to go outside. During the summer it would have been alright because the kids would have been outside all day.

I never had no job, no regular income. And Denby was just working on a farm as a labourer. He'd go away at six o'clock in the morning and come back at nine o'clock in the evening. We never saw him hardly. So I finally I said, "I'm going to move to Regina." I'd see if I could get a place. Even if I had to live on welfare for a little while I said I wouldn't mind just as long as I could get out of that house. So one day I came into town with my sister and we walked around until we found a place that a lady said she'd rent to us. It was a two-bedroom house and it was very small. The bathroom was downstairs and it had this real rickety stairs. It was $275 a month. I had saved some money from my job, enough to make the deposit and pay for a month's rent. When we moved in to town all we had was one mattress, a sleeping bag and our clothes. There was me, my kids, and I got a babysitter, Joanie, and her little boy. There was five of us. When we first moved in we made twenty dollars stretch for two weeks.

It was very convenient for me to have Joanie because I could go out in the day and look for a job and then go back in the evenings and cook supper. We had lots of wild meat from the reserve. Denby had killed a deer and about thirty rabbits. So we went out to the reserve every weekend and got all the meat we needed. My dad had a vegetable garden so he gave us potatoes. That's why twenty dollars lasted as long as it did.

Slowly by slowly we got it together. I went to Indian Affairs and told them I needed help and they gave me help for half a month. I put in an application for low-rent housing because I couldn't afford $275 a month. I went to the Friendship Centre and they sent me up to Native Women (Regina Native Women's Association) where I met Anna Crow. She said that they were hiring five women for a Canada Works program and she said "Are you interested in working?" I jumped at it. It was only minimum wage but it was something. I was fortunate because this was just a month after I had moved in. Since I had grade twelve I guess they thought here's someone who will at least do her job.

Then in June of '78 I got a low-rental house. Representatives from Native Women, the Friendship Centre, and a couple of other organizations sit on a selection board and when your name goes up before them they decide if you really need a house.

I quit Native Women for a while because it was just a temporary job. I took a girl's place who had just had a baby. She didn't want to come back to work because she thought she would be putting me out of a job. I thought it would be better if I quit and let her come back and have the job so I went on unemployment insurance for two months. Then this position came open and they phoned me, and asked if I would like to come back and work. It's an administrative training position. I do payroll, looking after the synoptics, book-keeping.

I have a different babysitter now. I have Mrs. Erikson; she's a really good babysitter. She's a white lady. It seemed funny for me to take my kids there but she really likes them, she's very good with them.

I'll probably have my baby in Regina but then I'll go back to the reserve for a while, to my parents. Then I'll come back. I can't stay too long off this job because I used most of my unemployment insurance up when I quit in December. I'm looking forward to coming back to work here even if it's just for the training. Even if I'm not here for fifteen years or something, if I got the training I could go somewhere else for a job and say that I had worked here for a year.

Denby did work in the city for a while on drywall contracting before he got the job with the Department of Highways. But he got ripped off so many times it's not even funny. They'd always have mix-ups with the guy who got the jobs for them. They'd hire guys like Denby to go in the houses and do the work. Then the guy would come by and say, "How long will this take you?" And they'd give him their hours and he'd go and he'd change them and they'd lose money that way. For the amount of work they did, it never really paid.

When they got a job they might start at seven o'clock in the morning and go to ten o'clock at night. The sooner they got it done, the sooner they got the money. They'd be working all day long but they just made enough to keep going. So he got fed up with that. He wanted to go back to the reserve too because he didn't like the city all that much. Not because it's not a nice place to live . . . well, it really isn't a nice place to live. At least not for me it's not.

I came in to Regina for grade ten so I had a little bit of an idea what it was like here. I enjoyed it when I was in grade ten because I had no responsibilities. I went to a show every weekend. I lived with my uncle and my aunt. It was good. I got ten high school credits. I only had one friend and she lived all the way across town so I got all my homework done. If I had been out on the reserve I wouldn't have got the credits or the high marks. Grade eleven and twelve I went back to Fort Qu'Appelle.

I'd rather see my kids grow up on the reserve but I'd want them to go to an integrated school. It makes you prepared for so much more. Coming to Regina if you've just gone to the reserve school you're not prepared for all these things. When I went to the integrated school there was lots of prejudice so I was prepared for it when I came in to Regina. It really hits you in the face. Like getting on the bus when you're the only Indian on the bus and everybody just stares at you. That's one thing. Another is when you go into a store, the detectives follow you around. You go to one place and this guy is standing there watching you. He doesn't hide it that he knows you are an Indian so he's just going to watch you. I guess they blame the high rate of stealing and shoplifting on Indians.

There's lots of street gangs in Regina now, it's getting really bad. My cousin came in to town from the reserve for the weekend and he and a group of friends were going to go out. They pulled in to this service station and this gang of kids pulled in beside them and started talking about them, razzing them and laughing at them. So my cousin said, "You can't do that" and they jumped out and started fighting and he got his leg broke. Right at a gas station. White gangs against native gangs. My cousin and his friends ended up in jail because they figured they were the ones that started it. They couldn't say anything against the other group. This happens quite a lot. This one person I was talking to said his mother is a seventy-one-year-old woman who got beat up by a gang of guys. She's an Indian woman and they were white. They beat her up because her grandchild wouldn't do something they wanted him to do. I think it's getting dangerous.

I used to take the bus to work and I bet you every day I'd have somebody stop me when I was waiting on the street and ask me if I want a ride or if I want to make twenty dollars, or "could I take you for a drink?" something like that. Not ugly old beat-up cars either, nice big new cars stopping us. I'll say "no" and I'll walk around the street and they'll follow me. Mostly middle-aged guys and they'll bother you when you're just going to work. I've got bothered so much it isn't even funny. Now I'll either get a ride to work or else take a cab.

Last week a friend of mine was walking down a street near here and a white guy stopped her and asked her if she'd like to do a trick, if she'd like to make twenty dollars. Three times he stopped her. So the last time she picked up a rock and she hucked it at him. She was trying to get it in the window but it hit the car door. She said if there .was a cop down the street he probably would have charged her with damaging property. I don't think that happens to white girls.

It's even getting scary on the reserve. When I was younger, my friend lived about a mile away and it would be nothing for me to walk along the road to her house. But now knowing how corrupt the reserve is getting and with the alcohol, it's getting dangerous. Young kids speeding down the road. I wouldn't walk with my kids down the road now; if I had to go anywhere, I would go across country. It's changing.

The younger kids are getting mature that much sooner, they're growing up so much faster. Lots of kids drop out of school after grade nine and then spend their time after that in the city, on the street; so they end up knowing a lot more than a lot of the older people about what the city is like. But they have nothing to look forward to; it seems like nobody's helping them. They get a dishwashing job or a waitress job, nothing that they can really work up on.

I can't say the city looks good to most people on the reserve because most of them have an idea of what the city's like already. But a lot of people have to move off the reserves because there is no housing and no jobs and you need an education. The good jobs on the reserve go to people who have had good educations and you have to go off the reserve to get that. Our reserve is thirty-six square miles and has over a thousand people. That's a lot of people squeezed on thirty-six square miles. It's good land but maybe only enough land for a few farmers.

A lot of people who have a hard time in Regina end up going back to the reserve. Like a mother, say, with three children who is just living on welfare. You can't improve yourself on welfare and you can do the same thing on the reserve.

Most people on our four reserves speak English. The parents are very strict about not teaching the kids on the reserve Indian language

because they are afraid that it will hold them back. A lot of old people are like that. When they went to residential schools they were beaten for speaking the Indian language. They believe that if their kids speak the Indian language they will be beaten too. And they don't want that. Now our generation who didn't get to learn this want to learn it. A lot of people are getting away from the culture too; they don't identify with what went on a long time ago because we've been cooped up on these reserves for so long. People have been so controlled by Indian Affairs. You couldn't even kill a cow or a chicken without a permit. And we're just starting to break out of that now.

I think that the cultural thing is really important. If our parents and grandparents had taught us to speak Cree and had taught us in the Indian way, I think we'd be better people. For my kids, I want to send them to a Cree school and also get an elder to come and live with us for a few years and teach us all. There's so many things in our culture if we had known them when we started to grow up it would be so much easier now. In our culture a man could never hit a woman. But now it's changed all around, men are beating up on their women. And a man would never think of taking on a woman unless he was capable of looking after her. In our culture you would never hit a child unless you would just use a little twig and hit him on the back of the leg. You would never hit him on the face or the body. Old people treated young people as if they were the same age as them. Nobody was higher or lower. All you see now is that adults are higher than children or teenagers are higher than children. And you see that lots of people are neglecting their children. In the city it's so easy to get alcohol and they get drunk and the children are there at home not eating.

These cultural things need to be introduced in

the city too. An Indian is an Indian anywhere as long as you remember that you are an Indian, and what you are supposed to be doing with your culture and your ceremonies. You profit more than if you all of a sudden drop it and try to turn white. That's when you start to face all the problems. But it's hard; these last fifty years there has been little training. We should listen to the older people. If they have some of the values and some of the heritage that was passed on from before, we should try to learn more from them. We should also borrow all the good traits from the white society and try to put them into ours. And they can learn from us. Some white people are interested, I know lots of younger people who are learning about our ceremonies and our language. But I'm just learning all these things too.

Two Families

The Paul Family

Wallace shows off his guns. First, a .222 rifle that he uses for elk in the bush and on the high ground east of the highway. He runs his hand gently along the smooth, fine-grained wood of the stock and passes the rifle to John Stag. John takes it and crinkles his old, scarred, road map of a face, and, squinting an eye, sights down the barrel at the leg of the television set. He nods. Wallace says he will sell the .222 to John when John gets his cheque. They set the rifle aside. Wallace gets up heavily from the table and goes into the other room, the room where the freezer sits, and brings out the other guns; the Winchester lever action he uses for deer, a small shotgun, an old .303 army rifle that he uses for moose. He points to the freezer and chuckles deep in his throat. The freezer is full of elk meat. He pats the .222.

Myrtle, Wallace's daughter, brings out three photographs of Beverly. All are in cardboard folders; Instamatic snap shots that have been blown up to eight inches by ten. In all three pictures the subject is standing outdoors; a pretty girl with a shy smile and eyes just barely looking up. Her dark hair is blown slightly to the side in the breeze. She is young in the pictures, eighteen, and still has a teenage figure. Along the bottom of the photographs is written in ink, "We miss you Bev." Beverly is dead. She was run over one night on the road outside Wallace's house as she and her brother and a couple of her sisters were walking home from the village. The guy driving the car was drunk. He lost his licence and received a twenty-five-dollar fine.

Wallace goes to a cupboard and brings out a manilla envelope and pulls out a life insurance policy for Beverly. It is from a company in Toronto. The pages of the policy are creased and worn; their black jumble of long words in tiny print have been pored over, figured over frequently without every yielding up any of their mystery.

"We were supposed to get $6000 when she died," says Wallace. "But somewhere it says that if you are killed when you are walking beside the road you only get $1500." He looks quizzically at the mass of words on the policy then folds it once more and puts it away.

Hilda says, quite matter of factly, that she likes the street they live on; it is quiet and there are "not many Indians". Hilda too is Wallace's daughter. College Avenue in Winnipeg is a whole street of little frame houses, moderately well kept. Stretching west from Main for four miles to the end of the city, it is a flat street with little shade in this flat, desert-like northwest expanse of the inner city. This is the true north end of Winnipeg with rows of tightly-packed, neat, working-class houses on uninteresting streets. The pattern of the houses is broken only by corner stores, school yards, and the occasional Lutheran or Ukrainian or Catholic church. This is lunch-bucket country, the home of the immigrant working class after they have ceased to be the unemployed poor and have become the working poor.

Hilda and her man, Stanley, have been living in the little blue house for several months. Stanley and Bill, a cousin who lives with them, have painted two of the rooms. But the roof still leaks over the back porch, and Stanley says that they will take the carpeting out because it is badly worn. The front door is locked, with signs in the window; "Go To Back Door" and "Beware of Dog" (though the dogs are a chihuahua and a German shepherd puppy).

The door is locked because the front porch is a bedroom; it has a single bed in it and maps of Manitoba and Winnipeg tacked to the wall. Inside are two bedrooms, a yellow-painted kitchen, and a living room with a chesterfield and a chair and an old Philco black-and-white television. On the wall in the living room hangs a rug with a woven scene from the Arabian Nights. Above the bedroom door is an enlarged photograph of Hilda and Stanley, smiling and hugging, taken by a photographer at the Red River Exhibition. Over the kitchen door hangs a plaque that says in plaster of Paris; "Christ Is the Head of this House, the Unseen Guest at Every Meal, the Silent Listener to Every Conversation." In the back porch the German shepherd puppy has pulled over the garbage and is going through it looking for chicken bones.

It is 160 kilometers from Wallace's house at Dog Creek on the east side of Lake Manitoba to the little house on College Avenue. The 160 kilometers is the distance between worlds and the shrinking distance between the two parts of one family's life. The distance is covered weekly in at least one direction by Wallace's big, heavy, rattling, covered-with-dust brown Pontiac station wagon. With Wallace in his sun glasses settled behind the wheel and the back filled with kids, it moves along the deeply rutted gravel road that winds through the reservation; through the marshy hay land, the oak, elm, willow, and black poplar stands; past high-perched Indian Affairs houses, overturned cars, washing machines sitting outside houses, dogs, horses, cows, children. At the curve in the road is the plywood sign advertising the southern entrance to the reserve; a sign with a decorative tipi painted onto it; a sign that has been used for target practise and has a hole the size of a soccer ball blasted out of the middle of it. Then it is 20 kilometers up the dusty provincial road to the highway and another 130 kilometers south to Winnipeg.

Dog Creek is the reserve base for the family; Wallace, his wife Grace, their collection of children and grandchildren. On the reserve they live with two houses, an old one built in 1965 and now in disuse, and a newer four-bedroom house built in 1975. The houses face each other across a rutted laneway, pulled off the road behind a clump of willows and beside a hayfield that stretches down to the lake. The blue frame house on College Avenue represents the family's tentative approach to the city. There twenty-six-year-old Hilda waits with Stanley, her two little boys, and whoever else from the family might be there at any particular time, for the arrival of the big brown station wagon.

I keep feeling like I am part of a scene that I remember from Alabama. I feel like I am on a back road where the Negros' houses stand, at intervals, between the dust of the road in front and the ferocious threat of the creeping undergrowth in back; standing in the steamy heat with dogs panting under the porches, women hollering at little black children who shinny up the unpainted porch poles, and men languishing in bib overalls and nothing else, waiting.

It is not Alabama, but I cannot escape the feeling. We sit avoiding the broiling sun only by making a brief pact with the ribbon of shadow that falls from the north eave of Wallace's house. We sit on cracked kitchen chairs on the baked ground of the yard drinking beer from bottles as the children rattle past on assorted tricycles and toys, while Grace and her daughters clean up in the house behind us. In the heat and the haze we savour the easy sociability of the beer and the callers who pull in off the road in dusty beaten vehicles and pause for twenty minutes or an hour and leave again. The talk rambles between English for my benefit and Saulteaux for the comfort of most of the other people there. Around us are the hayfields farmed by the three well-off families or leased to the diligent, meticulous Icelanders. And beyond, in the sun, stretches the reserve; the soggy marshlands bright green, with flocks of blackbirds periodically exploding like shotgun pellets and swirling above them. Beyond the marsh is the flat pale blue of the lake. Beneath the step the dog lies panting.

Lake Manitoba Reserve stretches, like a body half-curled in sleep, for twenty kilometers along the east shore of the lake from the Métis village of Vogar and the tourist highway that carries in American fishermen, south to the farms and ranches and the provincial road that goes out to the town of Eriksdale. At the centre of the reserve is a knot of buildings, almost a village, with the new Indian Affairs school, an arena and community centre, a Catholic church and graveyard, the band office, a garage, a small store. On either side of this centre, the houses are spattered sporadically along the road for the whole twenty kilometers.

Wallace and Grace were both born on the reserve. Wallace says that when he was young, the reserve had maybe three hundred people. Now he estimates there are more than six hundred. There are, according to official Indian Affairs figures, 595 band members, 410 living on the reserve. Wallace and Grace have had eleven children. Wallace has worked all over the country but for the last three years he has worked steadily on the reserve as the caretaker of the new school. A little ice fishing is done from the reserve on the lake in the winter; three families farm and run herds of white-face cattle; everyone else works for the band, like Wallace, on near-by farms owned by white farmers, or is on welfare.

It is impossible to understand the Paul family by thinking of individual people, individual lives. One needs to think of a group of people, a collection of bodies melded together into this family. A group of people of whom no count is automatically taken. No one, at any given time, could ascribe a number to those staying at the house on the reserve or at the house in the city without stopping first to count them off one by one.

If it is a family without count, it is also a family without bounds. A family where there is always room for an extra, where another body is welcomed without fuss or formality, where every other body moves over one space with a motion that is automatic and the new person is absorbed and accepted as if he or she had always been there.

Wallace is a heavy man, round, with a great girth. His fingers are stubby and fat. His hands are plump. He has a great neck and fat cheeks, yet he is not a fat man, does not move like a fat man. Wallace is a big, gentle man, not easily flustered, who likes to laugh. He chuckles at all the children around him and makes little jokes with his wife.

Despite the heat, Wallace in summer wears many of the same clothes he wears in winter. He wears a brown turtleneck under his brown outer shirt. He wears green work pants and work boots. On his head he has a baseball cap, blue and white with mesh sides for ventilation. He wears sunglasses. This is Wallace's uniform. I have rarely seen him dressed otherwise. He wears these clothes or similar ones for his job cleaning the school. He wears them on Saturday night when he visits the pub in Eriksdale, and on trips to the city. He will often keep his cap on when sitting in the house.

Grace, Wallace's wife for thirty years, is a small woman. It is easy to see how attractive she was when younger, though now she is worn from hard work and the bearing of eleven children. Her edges are sharper than Wallace's. She is quicker to anger and has a more focused wit. Sometimes she becomes angry with Wallace, but they are intensely loyal to each other, and to their children.

Hilda first came to Winnipeg eight years ago when her son, Harry James, was born and required intensive hospital care and a series of operations for intestinal difficulties. Stanley has been in the city on and off for six years. Hilda is capable and somewhat at ease in the city in spite of her sometimes painful shyness and the fact that she is less comfortable speaking English than she is speaking Saulteaux. Hilda is starting to get slightly heavy in her arms and thighs and through her middle.

Stanley is a slight man with a high bony forehead and long curly hair. Personable and self-possessed, he is the kind of man one feels will not be easy to get to know but the effort will be repaid. He is alert, with a cautious wisdom not unlike that of a wolf who watches the hunters baiting the traps meant for him.

Stanley comes from Bacon Ridge, the Métis town on the edge of the Ebb and Flow reserve on the west side of Lake Manitoba. He is non-status Indian. He has brothers who are treaty and who live on the reserve but he was never registered. He is the child of a status woman and a non-Indian man. As they were not married, he could have been registered on the reserve, but was not. He says he wishes he were treaty so he could live on a reserve and have a house there. He is torn between Winnipeg and the country. His mother lives in Winnipeg several blocks from the house he and Hilda have. He can make it around the city though he would prefer the country, but there is no living to be made there. At Ebb and Flow the men either do some ranching, work for the band or the community, or go away to work on construction or for the CNR.

Brothers, sisters, cousins are regularly part of Hilda and Stanley's household, staying a day, a week, or several months. Also there are the two little boys, Albert and Harry James. Nine and eight years old, Albert and Harry James play and tease and scrap and have made friends with the Chilean children who live across the street. Indoors they play with the German shepherd puppy, teasing it mercilessly, or they watch television.

The boys attend a small elementary school three blocks from the house. They used to go to a larger, older school close to the house but in the other direction, toward downtown, but Hilda worried about them. They were staying late after school; hanging around. Hilda was afraid they would get into trouble. "There were too many Indian kids there," says Stanley. One evening that school was broken into. Word came back quickly that though it was older boys who initiated the break-in, Albert and Harry James had been there. Hilda didn't know what to do; she and Stanley finally called the police. Then they had to watch achingly for thirty minutes while the police interrogated the two frightened little boys in the squad car. After that, Hilda moved the boys to the new school.

Stanley and Hilda both work at a small electric parts plant on Pacific Avenue, fifteen minutes by bus from their home. Hilda has been on welfare and this is the first job for her in a long time. She makes $3.10 an hour working with seven other women putting screws on electrical parts. Two of the other women are Indian, the rest are Philippinos and Poles. Stanley makes a dollar more an hour as a die cutter. He has worked at the plant before and says he gets on well. He gets up at 5:00 AM because he likes to drink his morning coffee slowly. They work from 7:30 AM until 4:00 PM.

Once, Hilda's fifteen-year-old brother David came to stay with them. He had come to make some money and Stanley and Hilda got him a job at the electric parts plant. He intended to work for a short while and then return to the reserve to go back to school. One night, late, he and two friends were walking home along Manitoba Avenue when David was jumped and beaten up by two men. His nose was broken, his wrist was cracked, and he was cut in the shoulder by a knife. His friends ran off into the night in fright and his attackers left him lying on the sidewalk. The next day David went back to the reserve.

The school at Dog Creek where Wallace is the caretaker is sprawling and new with a façade of sculpted grey concrete. The reserve is proud of the new school, as is Wallace. He takes a subtle delight in showing a visitor around, laughing at the miniature furniture in the kindergarten, apologizing for the mess in the library which is the librarian's, not his, responsibility to clean up.

During the school year he opens the door before eight o'clock in the morning and makes sure things like heat and plumbing are functioning adequately. But he does most of his work after three-thirty in the afternoon when the children have left. It is then that he cleans up, sweeping the mud out of the halls, re-ordering the chaos of the day's activities, making it all look again like new. He works on into the evening until it is all done.

Until some months ago, Grace was working with him part-time, helping him with the cleaning. But the band council laid her off. It is now too much work for Wallace alone. He is there until late each night. As well, without Grace's income, they are having a hard time making ends meet.

Now the family is in a quandary. The whole situation has made Wallace too irritated to do the caretaking any longer. He feels that there is more work than one person can do. At home the family has ten, sometimes twelve or fourteen mouths to feed. He is angry at the band which keeps having meetings trying to decide whether or not to hire Grace back. He has told them that if they don't hire her back he will quit as well. But if he doesn't do the caretaking, there is no other work for him on the reserve; at least not work offering comparable remuneration, status, and security. He doesn't know what to do.

The difficulties with the job cause the family to look with anger at other things around them they don't like. Wallace points to a rotted board under the linoleum inside the front door of their house. The house is starting to fall apart, he says. Grace complains about the cold in the house in the winter. She is dreading winter, another winter where they spend five hundred dollars for sixteen loads of wood for their heater and still have to leave the electric oven on with the door open on frigid nights. In the quandary, in the bitterness, they start to nurture fantasies about the city. Every time I see them, Wallace and Grace offer tentatively that they "think they might move to the city."

In Winnipeg Hilda and Stanley say that Wallace and Grace would not like it there; there would be no work for Wallace and Grace would be driven to distraction trying to keep all the little children off the street. But they admit there is little they can say to their parents about it. Hilda says that her parents would miss the social life of the reserve, as she does, and would be lonely. She and Stanley say they seldom go out socially; just to work, shop, or to visit Stanley's mother. Hilda's social life revolves around her family during the frequent times that Wallace and Grace drive in to Winnipeg and stay at her house. She and Stanley go up to the reserve less frequently. They don't have a car, though they would like to get one before winter. There are other people from Dog Creek in Winnipeg but they don't socialize with them. They don't use any of the facilities of the native organizations; the Friendship Centre, etc.; and don't know anyone else who does. They have a vague notion of what goes on there but suggest that most Indian people see those facilities as quite exclusive.

Every once in a while a tinge of homesickness or longing slips into Hilda's conversation. She says that the city is good in the winter but that in the summer she gets very restless. When she was younger, Hilda was married and left Dog Creek to live on a reserve on the other side of the lake. When she was divorced from her husband the band council at the Lake Manitoba reserve had to give their consent for her to move back there and have her own house. The permission was never given. She wasn't refused but neither did anyone make a favourable decision. Without the band council's permission she can never get a residence at Lake Manitoba. Now with Stanley being non-treaty, the complications involved in her possible return are even greater.

The Piché Family

Imagine a picture from a family album, a snapshot pulled from the chaos of events; a picture that freezes the smiles awkwardly on faces and holds a moment suspended in a sort of off-balanced limbo, out of context of all other events, all moments, and all history. It is 1967 in the picture, Centennial year. There are a woman, a man, and three children. The oldest child is a little girl around ten, with pigtails and long skinny legs. A younger child, a little boy who lugs a wooden gun beside him casually as if it might be a rag doll, is perhaps five, and the smallest, a girl, looks to be about three. They are standing beside a car. Inside are suitcases and boxes. Beside the car, the man looks stern. Above him the aspen leaves are rippling silver in the wind that picks up off the lake. The woman stands beside him, one foot ever so slightly ahead of him; she touches his sleeve lightly, imperceptibly. Her face is flushed with a tight frightened smile. Her eyes are bright.

The woman's name is Aldina. The picture snapped, she moves to retrieve the camera from the elderly man, her father, who laughingly asks for reassurance that he has been holding it right side up. The old man is already in his seventies; a big man and a strong man, not as limber as he once was although he still goes into the bush north and east of the lake to set his traps and attend to them in the late fall and the early spring. The woman touches him quickly and the old woman who stands beside him. Then she turns. The children are already being hustled into the car, clambering over the boxes. They shout their good-byes through the windows. Grimly the man turns the key and the motor catches. It roars. A puff of dust and a shrivelled dead leaf moved by the exhaust touch the shoes of the grandparents. The gears rasp; the car moves. The people wave, but they are silent. It is less than two hundred miles away, this place they are going to. But there are many things they don't know. How will it be when they see each other again? Will they be able to move with the same easy familiarity into the house, into their roles, into each other's worlds? Or will they be different people? Will the lake still strike the same joyous feeling of belonging when they see it lying still and misty in the early morning? Will the children want to come back? Will they come back to "home", or will they come back as tourists? The car turns south on the gravel road and then southwest on the highway. They are silent except for the three-year-old who sings absently to herself.

Aldina is forty-two. She is a strong but strangely fragile woman, hauntingly pretty, vulnerable, with softness in her face and deep dark eyes. She is also tough.

Twelve years after the snapshot was taken, we meet in a suite of olive-coloured offices in the basement of a new building on a nondescript street of dry cleaners, convenience food stores, and three-storey walk-up apartment buildings just north of downtown Edmonton. Aldina leans back in her high-backed black leather chair. She is self-possessed, comfortable. For six years she has worked here on a program to promote the hiring of native people in jobs throughout Alberta, especially in the burgeoning construction and oil development areas of the north and northeast. Now she is a co-ordinator of the program. She is at ease with her position, coolly in control whether she is talking on the phone, handling visitors, or travelling; tomorrow she goes to Rocky Mountain House for a meeting, the next day to Grand Centre to participate in the making of a film. The other workers moving constantly in and out of her office defer to her experience and ability. They talk about her tenaciousness in getting the project going and keeping it going.

Aldina is no longer the hesitant, frightened woman standing with every muscle in her face tense, waiting to get in the dusty car and start the pilgrimage. She has met the world head-on, and she has carved out her place in it, but the world has left its mark on her in return. There is a part of Aldina Piché that has been hurt. She scrambles to cover it up with little jokes that are self-deprecating but tinged with bitterness and cynicism. The clues are all there; the absence of pure joy, the wisdom of sorrow, the forced displays of toughness. Her language is spicy. Sometimes she talks like a longshore-man — "Goddamns" and "bastards" thrown in with ease and possibly with relish but often only to reassure herself. Back of it all there is a discernable trembling in this gentle, likable, approachable, and not even particularly wary woman.

We are interrupted by a tall skinny boy wearing an enormous black cowboy hat who comes into the office and is introduced as Darren, her son. Aldina gives him ten dollars and the keys to her car. He is off north to Cold Lake. "It is still home," she says to me, "Edmonton is alright but that reserve is still home."

Aldina's identity as an Indian is more than simply a racial identity; it is a chosen professional identity. You could call her, if you like, a professional Indian. She works with Indians, she lobbies for them, for jobs and for training. She goes to work as an Indian. When she meets government, labour, business people, she meets them as an Indian speaking on behalf of Indian people, Indian issues. When she makes her way through the bureaucracies of the city and the province, she does so as an official Indian. When she sits on the committees and the boards of directors of social services and organizations and when she goes to conferences it is as an Indian, as a representative of her project which is an Indian project. She has an official identity that has melded with her personal identity.

The first time Aldina came to Edmonton, she was sixteen. She came with a white girlfriend to find work. She applied for work at a hospital but knew from the moment she walked in that she wasn't going to be hired. She ended up working as a domestic, a maid for an American family who had her wear a uniform and eat in the kitchen but who took her along to church with them on Sundays. She was desperately homesick but determined to stay on for as long as she could. She lasted for eight months.

Aldina went to residential school to grade eight and is self-taught beyond that. The school was run by nuns whom she remembers as fierce and unrelent- ing women who told the children that they were "pagans". "We prayed all the time," she recalls, "always on an empty stomach." She claims that they were taught only about church history, Latin, and how to get to Heaven. She tells about being wakened with the rest of the children in the middle of a winter's night because the school barn was on fire. The sisters herded them, half asleep, into the chapel to pray for the barn. It burned anyway. "I don't want to say that it was all bad," she adds quickly. "One thing we learned for certain there was discipline."

In the northwest corner of growing, sprawling Edmonton, the houses lie back a discreet distance, hidden from the roar of the traffic, the Gulf self-serve stations, the Ponderosa steak houses, and the Sears warehouses. The houses are all bungalows or one-and-a-half storeys, vintage 1960, with small flower beds and ornamental trees on the front lawns.

Aldina's house is a bungalow with a front walk that winds between two huge blue spruce trees. Snapdragons and marigolds grow clustered in a small bed by the steps. The front of the house is faced, around the large living room window, with clapboard painted blue. The sides of the house are stuccoed. The front door opens into the living room with its rust shag carpet, a couch, a television set, and a chair where a black and white cat lies asleep. On the wall is a framed Eskimo tapestry, two white figures bent over a hole in the ice attempting to pull up the body of a harpooned seal. Books and magazines are scattered about. There is a low coffee table with a deck of cards spread out where Darren has been playing a restless game of solitaire. A shelf of encyclopedias stretches neatly, formally, beneath a large mirror.

The dining room is brightly lit. An electric clock with spikes sticking out from around its face stares down from the wall at an oval Arborite table. Aldina and Kathy sit at the table packaging blueberries from last week's trip to Cold Lake. They work quickly, the dark, plump berries rolling down between their fingers. The blueberries are cleaned of their leaves and stems, washed, put in plastic bags, and placed in the freezer in the small blue kitchen. Aldina chuckles that she takes off to pick berries in August "like every good Indian." This has been a good year. The berries are fat and plentiful and the bears have left enough for everybody else. Aldina is in a good mood, tossing jokes at Kathy. She gets up to make tea. Kathy searches in her mother's freezer for space for one more package of berries. On the table there is still part of a basket to be done. Aldina looks at the berries and cautions not to waste any lest these be the last they get. Once the oil gets going at Cold Lake, she speculates wryly, it will probably ruin the berries.

As Aldina brings in the tea, the house and the night seem to close in around us. She and Frank bought the house eleven years ago, she says, on a special mortgage and down-payment loan for "off-reserve housing" from the Department of Indian Affairs. It was worth $16,500 then and in the current Edmonton market is probably worth $65,000.

Kathy is twenty-two, a slim young woman with flawless olive skin and lustrous black hair combed back and parted in the middle. She is slim in a delicate, fragile, China-doll kind of way with small hands. The ring finger of her left hand wears a modestly cut diamond. She wears large gold-framed glasses.

Kathy works for the RCMP as a file clerk. She is the first — and the only — Indian person to work in the Alberta headquarters — a sprawling bowling alley of a building at the edge of an industrial part of the city. She was the only Indian on the floor at her previous job with the Canada Employment and Immigration Commission in Edmonton. She says that it is not easy to be the only Indian in a workplace and says that she is aware of people who work with her who stereotype her. To her it means that they, in very subtle ways, don't expect her to last. She says that she used to go out of her way to be friendly with such people in an attempt to allay their fears or to have them like her. It wasn't worth the trouble. Now she says that she ignores them. Yet she feels a constant and unrelenting obligation to prove herself.

Kathy and her mother share a deep affection. The two joke with each other and tell stories. Kathy is the only one of the children who really remembers the reserve, having lived there until she was ten. She would like to live on the reserve sometime in the future, she says, perhaps transferring to the RCMP office at Grand Centre. First she wants to spend time in the city learning more on her job and perhaps attending university. Now she lives alone in an apartment a mile from her mother's house.

Darren is seventeen, very shy, almost sullen. He is lanky, skinny in blue jeans, sneakers, jean jacket, T-shirt. He has long curly black hair and a wild, somewhat frightened face. He is going through a difficult time now, Aldina has said. He drives her car into the ground and drinks. He has quit school and spends the winter playing hockey for a team on a reserve a half-hour's drive from the city. In the summer he works off and on for a paving company. They work him for fourteen hours in a day and pay him seven dollars an hour. Then they won't call him up for a week. So he lies around the house or drives around in Aldina's car. Aldina complains that since his father left there is no one around to step hard on a teenaged boy. Then she mutters, almost as an afterthought, that she was the only one who ever disciplined the kids anyway.

Becky is fifteen. She is active, almost tomboyish,

with bobbed, tousled hair. She lives for athletics, always at baseball practice or basketball practice. She plays for an all-Indian girl's basketball team called the Skyhawks. Aldina shows a scrapbook filled with photos and clippings of Becky's exploits. There is a great series of photos from a trip the Skyhawks recently made to Utah. Becky is in grade eleven but is indifferent to school; sports is her love.

Aldina and Frank are now separated. Not much is said about Frank. I know about him only obliquely, comments that Aldina lets slip, things people who have known them both have said. Since the marriage broke up, Frank moves back and forth between the city and Cold Lake. Sometimes he still stays at the house. When at Cold Lake he moves back into the cabin that the family used as a summer cottage during their regular visits back home from Edmonton.

Aldina continues to grope through the closets of her mind and memory for clues and meanings to the separation. Frank's departure leaves a silent hole in the family, one that isn't talked about easily. It was twenty-two years ago that Aldina and Frank were married. Twenty-two years is a long time, a lot of history.

Frank is Chipewyan, Aldina is Cree. Theirs was an odd marriage in that regard. His people are the majority at Cold Lake, hers only a scattered few. Neither has ever been able to speak the other's language. So they communicated always and only in English. The children learned only English. Kathy laughed once that at stormy moments in the marriage her parents would shout at each other cajoling one another to "teach the children some Indian language". Then they would fall into silence. Being from different nations forced them into the only common ground, the language of the whites.

With the benefit of hindsight, with the sorrowful knowledge of how much easier it is to stay than to leave even when you know that something is falling apart, with insights into human self-deception, Aldina talks about how she should have known for a long time that her marriage was crumbling. But she still doesn't know *why*. She flashes momentarily and blames the city, saying that "in Indian ways you were married for life". Then she pauses and looks away. "It's not the city, it's the times," she says. She is not like the young girls, barely women, whom she used to counsel years ago when she worked with the public health nurse. Those were hungry and terrified girls trailing into the city to escape young husbands they'd hardly had a chance to know. Aldina is not like them. She was married twenty-two years! It's not just happening to her, it's happening to her friends as well; women who came to the city when she and Frank did, women who, as girls, slept in the beds next to hers in the residential school. It's happening to them and it's happening to white people. It is surely the times. But that makes it no easier.

Aldina recalls her time in Edmonton. When she and Frank and the children came in 1967 Frank was going to apprentice as a technician for a firm that made aircraft instruments. They came to the city and took a cramped basement flat in a house where the landlord lived on the main floor. Aldina felt that she had to spend most of her time keeping the children quiet so that their playing wouldn't disturb the landlord. Darren was determined to climb the two dainty apple trees in the tiny back yard. He couldn't understand why this wasn't allowed — on the reserve there had been a million trees to climb.

They had few friends, although one of Aldina's sisters lived in Edmonton, and they didn't go out much. Frank brought home $400 a month and Aldina took a job in the kitchen of a hotel on weekends. They got by.

In the early years she was depressed and discouraged. "I told Frank I wanted to go home; I didn't care about the conveniences, I'd chop wood." He said, "no, we'll stick it out."

Frank worked for the aeronautical firm for five years but never got his papers because he didn't pass the theoretical parts of his examinations. He had only grade seven. After two lay-offs, he left and took a job with the Alberta Indian Association working to improve medical services on isolated reserves.

Aldina remembers going to pick blueberries when she was young and her father would take a five-gallon pail along to dip tar from the pools of thick black liquid that were to be found in the bush. He carried the tar home to brush on the roof of his chicken coop. Now Imperial Oil wants the tar.

Cold Lake is one of those names that now evokes visions of boom. It is, in fact, closely tied to Edmonton psychically. Its boom, or impending boom, is a part of the composite reason for Edmonton's boom. The bush is being cleared and the first wells are being sunk for the Cold Lake of the future. By the early 1980s Imperial Esso Resources will have a six-billion-dollar heavy oil processing plant well under way at Cold Lake. Cold Lake in the resources lexicon ranks with Fort McMurray and the Mackenzie Valley. It is the latest and biggest in a string of Eldorados that elicit all the superlatives the public relations departments of the oil industry and the Alberta government can manage.

The development activity is rapidly changing Cold Lake and its sister community, Grand Centre, from sleepy little ranching towns on the edge of a lovely clear little lake into exploding communities of bulldozer-scarred hillsides littered with the skeletons of new hotels and split level houses on forty-thousand-dollar lots. Every day now, one can fly three hundred kilometres from Edmonton to Cold Lake on little planes loaded with real estate speculators poring over street survey maps.

Actually the oil and Esso Resources is Cold Lake's second boom. The first was in 1954 when the Department of Defence put in the country's second largest air force base. That gives the community its character; two little ranching towns six kilometers apart — Cold Lake, population one thousand; Grand Centre, population three thousand — the air base, population six thousand, and the possibility that the oil plant will triple the population of everything. Up in the hills, in three communities that are all part of the Cold Lake Indian reserve, live one thousand Indians — Aldina and Frank's family and relatives.

For the Indians it was the air force base that made all the difference. The Department of Defence bought up huge areas of land around Cold Lake that had been Indian trap lines. They built the air base and used the former trap-line territory for target bombings.

The Indians collected their compensation and went on welfare. That's when Aldina and Frank started getting ready to leave. Aldina says; "Any self-respecting person had to leave; things were getting so violent, there was so much drinking." A social worker in Edmonton says that the streets of Edmonton's skid row and the cells of Alberta jails are still littered with the human wreckage from the Cold Lake of that time. Twenty-five years, and some people have never recovered.

But the Indian community has slowly recovered. Some people who stayed took hold of things. Aldina's parents stayed; one of Frank's cousins is now chief. The three communities that make up the reserve look placid enough stretched out over the rolling hills and poplar groves along the dirt roads that snake up from the two towns. The band operates a corporate ranch, a pre-fab plant to put together its own houses, and has a feisty, stubborn reputation as the band that pulled its children out of school for eight months in 1974 to back demands for a new reserve school. They got it. As for oil development, while they are not welcoming it, they are hoping to make the best of it. The band has formed a corporation that builds roads and is taking contracts to clear bush for Esso. When the jobs start they hope to have their young men and women ready to take their share of them and they are already involved in negotiating quotas with the major contractors and with Esso Resources.

Ironically, or perhaps not so ironically, it is Aldina's project that is encouraging and making the arrangements for the job training that will make surveyors, carpenters, welders, stenographers, machinery operators, engineers, and bookkeepers out of Cold Lake Indians who want in on the action.

Aldina says that she might live up in Cold Lake, on the reserve again. Her father died in the fall of 1979 at the age of eighty-four. Her mother still lives on the reserve, speaking little English, hating the thought of the city. Aldina fantasizes about giving it all up and going back; back to the peaceful lake or to some illusion of it.

Kathy would go back. Darren goes back in his wanderings. Frank goes back when he has nowhere else to go. The pull is strong, possibly stronger than the job. Stronger than the conveniences and the attractions; stronger than the house in the suburban northwest of Edmonton. Cold Lake. After a dozen years the reserve is still home.

Emil Simon, Regina

Emil Simon has buzzed into town from Victoria in his yellow Volkswagen. He is back in Regina to see a girlfriend, to give her a painting he has done, and to call in at old haunts, including the assorted native agency offices above the Friendship Centre on Toronto Street. Emil used to teach life skills here to a group of young natives associated with the Regina Plains Community College.

Born on the Hobbema Reserve south of Edmonton, Emil left home and the reserve in 1968 when he was eighteen. For the next ten years he travelled around between Calgary, Edmonton, the coast, Regina, and various oil and construction sites. Emil is a self-assured, neat, well-groomed man with frizzy hair parted in the middle. He wears tinted glasses, a black shirt and pants, and a grey tweed jacket. Around his neck is a silver arrowhead. He chews gum and smiles a lot with an effervescence that borders on that of the huckster. But he is likable. He is out to conquer the world by motion, footwork; good-natured but speedy. He has a fantasy of making an Indian movie with a hero that Indians can see as a model and whites can see as an example of a complex but self-sufficient and resourceful Indian human being.

My parents lived on the reservation, but my old man worked on the section [CN rail gang] so he was only home some of the time. But we lived on the reservation as kids. I stayed at my grandmother's a lot when I went to school. Then until I was sixteen I went to boarding school. It was a Catholic school run by priests and nuns. I so much wanted to go to a white school, but my parents never let me. They said that's a different thing than we were; this is where we belong.

I got into trouble with the law when I was quite young. When I was seventeen I did six months in jail for stealing a car. Then I came out and I went to work. My first job was at Juniper Lodge in Lacombe. I worked there until October. Then I went back to school, to a composite high school that was ten miles from Hobbema. I stayed with my uncle and used to take the school bus to go to school. Then I went back to jail; stole a car again. This was in '68. When I came out this time, my parents bought me a car so I wouldn't go around stealing them.

I went to work for this trailer factory that was ten miles from Hobbema. I worked there, I used to get paid every week and just blow it. But by that fall I had decided that for me to get into a better position in the working force I would have to have more education. So I applied to take an upgrading program at Red Deer College that fall. I got into college, but I also got thrown into jail for another six months for smoking — at that time smoking was in. Pot and stuff. I was into that so I got busted and I got thrown in for six months.

When I got paroled I went back to college right away. I finished there; I got all my high school and I got my first year psychology and sociology. I was pretty happy then. But then I got into drugs again. I got really into it this time. I was drinking and doing a lot of chemicals. And I got into speed. It didn't take long, I guess, maybe two months or three months before I was just completely zonked out. I spent two and a half months in the funny farm.

The funny thing was that when I was back on the reservation I always wanted to be the "white guy". So when I was going to the integrated high school, I always used to dress sharp. I would never wear the same clothes twice. I didn't want to look dirty, you know. I wanted to feel "look you

guys, I'm just as good as you if not better." A lot of people thought I was rich. It kind of made me feel good. Sometimes I'd go to school with no lunch. But as long as they were fooled, that was okay.

I think there were four of us who were Indian going to the college at Red Deer. But a lot of people didn't know I was Indian; they thought I was Mexican or Chinese. If they said, "Are you Mexican?" I'd always say, "Yeah," I'd never say I was an Indian. I had an inferiority complex. That, I think, I got from my parents because they'd say, "Don't play with those white kids" when we were small. I always wanted to ask them why we couldn't play with them, what's wrong with them or what's wrong with us.

When I went to the mental institution it was always in my mind that I had to make a better life for myself; I didn't want to be a drunken Indian or a lazy Indian. This was always in my mind because this was what I had heard somewhere else.

I met a girl in Calgary, a white girl. I thought, "this is an opportunity that is good, now I will have a white girl." Never mind the Indian girls. We started living together. I had a job, a construction job that paid good money. She was working. She taught me a lot of things about the white society, how to live in the city. We'd go to a fancy restaurant; I'd never been to a real plush place before. In Wetaskiwin they've got the Stanley Café. All the Indians eat there so it's like home. But we'd be going to the Calgary Inn or Blackbeard's or some really fancy place where there were no jeans allowed, and there'd be two forks on the table. I'm asking myself, "Why are these people giving me two forks?" She would teach me stuff like that and certain things that I'm not supposed to do — like burp at the table! I started getting adjusted into it all and I was starting to feel good, I was starting to feel like a white man because I was always with her friends. But I was always trying to show somebody something.

Usually everywhere I worked I got along with everybody. I never had any enemies; I seemed to adapt into whatever it was. I worked in gas plants. I worked at a Gulf refinery in Edmonton. After that I went to Calgary and worked at a Shell gas plant out there. Then I started driving taxi; it made me feel better, it takes experience to drive a taxi, I thought, and that made me feel good. Then I went to work for another construction outfit. I did all kinds of work; I worked for the handi-bus association in Calgary. Then I got into real estate. And I thought, "Hey this is it, you're with the big boys when you're into real estate." So I worked for Block Brothers and it was really interesting. I'd wear a tie and a white collar and stuff like that and be with the big boys. I used to eat up on the tenth floor at the cafeteria talking to big businessmen.

But I still felt out of place for some reason. I don't know. This was in '76. I moved to Fort St. John and went to work for Dow Chemical of Canada. I got the job in Calgary and I moved to Fort St. John and I worked as a truck driver. I got along with everybody and I didn't have any enemies. But I got into booze and I got my licence suspended so they had to let me go. So I went to work for McLeod's department store. Every time I got a good job; never had any problem with getting a job. Then I got hired on as a child-care worker in Fort St. John. After I worked there for a while I was approached by the Friendship Centre. Now this is my first contact with any Indian organization. They approached me in the fall of '76 and said, "We'd like to hire you, we've heard a lot of good things about you." So I said, this is great, everybody's asking me to do all this. So I went to work for the Friendship Centre as a legal informa-

tion worker. This is where I got stuck with working with native people. Before I used to think, "If that Indian over there can't work, it's not my fault. There's no reason for me to give him ten cents if he can't go to work like me. Why should I work my ass off and have him come around bumming from me? If I can make it so can he." This was my philosophy about the rest of the Indians. This was how I had always thought since I got into the white society because I had to make it one way or another. There was no way I was going to live on the reservation. But at this job I used to travel to reservations; three reservations twice a week. And I saw the conditions they were in. And I thought, geez, these guys are really having a rough time.

My job was to be a mediator between the native people and the law. I had no jurisdiction to act on anyone's behalf. The natives want to know some kind of law, and they would come and ask me. I go up there and find out what it is and then I go back and I tell them what it's all about. If it has anything to do with income tax, filling out forms and stuff like that, I could do it. I took a crash course on income tax and unemployment insurance. I also worked with the fish and wildlife people concerning the rights of native people. For instance, one lady got her fishing net taken away. She phones me and says, "I want to know why." So I says, "Okay, I'll get the information for you." So I go to the wildlife people, get the information, bring it back, and tell her the reason why they took her net away. "Now, anything you wanta do against the Fish and Wildlife is your business, not mine. The only thing I can do is suggest a few of the lawyers you might see if you want to charge these people."

The lady who hired me saw that I was starting to get along. I was starting to meet big people in the town. I knew the mayor, I knew the aldermen, I was getting to know the MLA. I was starting to set up some programs for native people and she was starting to fall out of the picture. So she fired me. And I believe still today that the reason she fired me was because she was jealous.

I took it to the Board of Directors and after looking at it they said, "We don't see any evidence of irresponsibility on your part, you can stay." A whole slew of them said that. But then the president said, "Hold on, we have to get the story from the executive director's side." So they called her back in and she said, "If you hire him back, I'll quit. I just can't work with him anymore." So the minute she said that, the president said, "If she quits I quit." So they let me go. I had failed. Right then and there I said to myself, "These fuckin' Indians. They'll stick it to you every goddamn time." I don't know why. Ever since then I've thought this is the last time I'm going to work for these Indians. You try to do them good and they shit on you. If you're a bum they still shit on you. What the hell are you supposed to do? So I went and got a job in a tire store.

Then this program on life skills came up, a workshop for four days that cost a hundred bucks. So I took it. These were all professional people who were in the group; teachers and social workers. And I was just nobody. I had no standing as far as people were concerned. So I was really nervous when we started the program. But then later on in the program somebody said that they thought I put things across really good, that they could really understand me. That made me feel really good; that program made me more aware of myself as an individual, not as an Indian, but as an individual. I'm human, they're all human. Some guys will try to do a lot of things to show off. And here I am trying to hold back some of the good

things I may have. So that brought everything back to an equal; you guys are okay, I'm okay. I'm a human, an individual, and so are all you people. So that sort of changed my whole line of thinking. Then I took the coaching training for life skills and have been working with that ever since.

When I was young I always wanted to live with and act like whites. But I changed with something I heard somebody say. They said, "Once you're an Indian, you're an Indian. You can never be a white man no matter what you do." This was when I started working with the Friendship Centre. I thought helping native people would be a good way to help identify myself. And I saw them in the situation they were in. At Fort St. John they were about twenty-five years behind everybody else. It was disgusting. These guys couldn't really go out and help themselves no matter what they did because they didn't have an education. They were just going to be pushed around. And in order to get out of that rut, they had to be helped. Not with money, but with telling them, "Look there's certain ways to go about getting yourself out of this rut. You have to fight with words, not with guns. And you can't just agree with somebody because it sounds good, you have to check it out." That's how I got started but it wasn't until I finished the life skills coach training in Edmonton that I really felt good about being an Indian. I thought, "Hey I'm an Indian, and I can identify proudly with being an Indian." If somebody called me a dirty lazy sonofabitchin' redskin I could say, "You really have a problem because it bothers you and it doesn't bother me." I would say, "If you want to keep thinking that way that's your problem, not mine."

Not all Indians feel this way. When they come from the reservation they feel a little inferior to the white man because the white man has everything. Some of the prejudice or always being put down has an effect. Ever since we were growing up we always heard from day one, "You're no damn good." When my mother would always tell me not to play with the white kids but would never tell me why I thought maybe I'm not as good. That's when I started to think that I'd have to be good just like them or better than them. I was always trying to compete with white people while I was growing up and I would not identify with Indians, unless somebody would say, "You're an Indian aren't you?" and I would say, "Yeah." But I would always stay away from that, if nobody mentioned it, I wouldn't mention it. Then when I took the program I started feeling good about being an Indian but I didn't go overboard and say, "Look, I'm an Indian and I'm better than you." I'm proud to be Indian, but I have to live with the white society, it's here to stay. So the only thing I can do is work with them and be happy at the same time because there's no way I can get away from it. I don't mind it because I use their conveniences; the car, the heating system, the houses. I use all these things. The only thing they can get from me is probably the heritage, you know, the culture.

I don't think I'd want to go back to the reservation. My family all feel that way; my sister has a good job in Calgary, she's a secretary, she's making a good living. My mother lives in Calgary. She's on welfare but it's a better living than living out on the reserve. The only one that's on the reserve is my brother. He must like living on the reserve. But for myself, I would never go and live there because I've seen too much of the Indian people pulling each other down. Why they do it I don't know. It's like the story where the white man and the Indian man are walking along and each has a pail full of crabs. The white guy has a lid on his pail but the Indian guy just has an open pail. Still, his crabs don't jump out. When the white guy asks him why his crabs don't jump out, he answers, "That's easy; they're Indian crabs. Whenever one of them gets near the top the others grab hold of him and pull him back down." There's too much jealousy. If somebody gets a new car, it doesn't matter that he might have worked his ass off to get it, the other people start asking, "Why does that guy have a new car? What does he think he is, a white man?" They just can't seem to understand that if that guy made it they shouldn't pull him down, they should praise the guy. The guys who make it should be an inspiration to the rest but it doesn't work that way. I don't know why.

The Indian is ahead of the white people in that he has two sets of values. He has to understand that one set is for life on the reservation and the other is for life here in the city. The Indians need those two sets of values.

This is the first time in my life that I have to make decisions for myself, now that I've split up from my wife. It's unfortunate to have to learn so late. In boarding school, where I was for nine years, all the decisions were made for you; you had to eat at this time, you had to go to church at this time, you had to wear this and do this and do that. Then after that I went to jail for a couple of years. That again was a time when there was no decisions that I had to make; you do this, you do that. If I didn't like to do something I still had to do it, or else. Then when I met my wife she made the decisions because I allowed her to because she was white. All that put me in the position where if something went wrong, it wasn't my fault. I could blame somebody else. Now that I'm alone I have to make my own decisions. I can't run to my mother. That's been a big change in my life. In the last year there's been a lot of changes in my life. I hope there's going to be a lot more.

Three Cities

Regina

There are no Indians in Regina

If you believe the Regina Real Estate Association, there are no Indians in Regina. In 1977 the Real Estate Association distributed publicity about its city, presumably in order to attract the interest of persons who might wish to locate there. Among the information in the brochure was an ethnic description of Regina that broke the population down proportionately by ethnic group. It listed the British, the Germans, the Ukrainians, the French, and so on. At no point did the list mention people of native ancestry. This was in spite of the face that the commonly used estimates of native people in Regina run between fifteen and twenty-five per cent of the city's population. And yet the numbers in the brochure added up to one hundred per cent.

It was a curious attempt by one group in the Queen City to overlook or deny the presence of Indian people. For in Regina, more than in any other city in Canada, the urban Indian is obvious. Regina is a small city — 149,593 people in 1976; a projected 160,513 in 1981. Out of that population conservative estimates by Ken Svenson, a researcher for the Department of Indian Affairs, put the native population at 13.7 per cent or 20,669 in 1976 and a projected 27,151 or 17 per cent in 1981. By 1986 the native population of Regina should grow, according to Svenson, to 36,491 or 21.2 per cent of a total population of 172,230. These figures, cautiously given, are consistently lower than the numbers ranging up to 25 per cent that are used by many other persons and organizations both native and white in Regina. This population, though smaller in absolute numbers than that of other cities like Winnipeg and Edmonton, is the highest, proportionately, of any Canadian city. So in Regina an Indian person is noticed; he or she doesn't easily melt into the background even should he want to.

Regina is a curious city. It was founded on the not unreasonable premise that there ought to be another city on the Canadian prairies between Winnipeg and the Rockies. So in 1882 Regina sprang to life, hammered together at a point where the CPR crossed the little Wascana Creek, on as flat a stretch of ground as can be found anywhere, with a soil that bakes hard as concrete in the summer and turns to mud in the rain. The unlikely spot, wrote Captain John Palliser in 1873 had "water but very little grass, a few willows but not wood fit for fuel." The site was remarkable, however, for an enormous pile of buffalo bones that in 1878 was reported to be thirty to forty feet high covering two or more acres of ground. Wascana or "Oscana" Creek, in fact, was so named by the Cree to mean "Pile o'Bones". There are varying theories that the bones were simply waste from years of the great buffalo hunts, that they had a quasi-religious significance to the Indian people, or that they marked the site where a peace pact had been agreed upon among several Indian tribes. (Edward McCourt, *Saskatchewan*, Macmillan of Canada, 1968) Both Algonkian peoples and the Sioux were known to frequent the area, among them tribes of the Cree, Assiniboine, Crow, Blackfoot, and Saulteaux. But with the coming of the railway all changed. By 1883 there remained at the spot no more than two or three cartloads of bones, and by 1886 nothing. All had been transported away to Minneapolis to make fertilizer.

Regina grew in order to service the developing farmland with railway activity, a growing territorial government that became a provincial government in 1905, a college for the Mounted Police, and a university. With a certain amount of pretention it was named in honour of Queen Victoria. The Queen, and her consort Albert, also got their names on the city's main streets. The city fathers laid out parsimonious lots in the downtown that fronted on narrow streets; they planted trees and later dammed Wascana Creek. The land around continued to open up to farmers. The city became a lively and a booming place.

The Indians, who had not long before piled the detritus from their buffalo hunts on the flats by the creek, pulled back; but then they too started to venture into the town. At the 1895 territorial fair the Indians made such a hit with their vigorous pow wows, displays of handicraft and farm produce, and with the performances of four brass bands made up of Indian boys from a local industrial school, that the tribesmen were admitted free to all the shows, and the Governor General, Lord Aberdeen, had medals specially struck for the boys in the bands.

Regina was and is a farm city, peopled by retired farmers and their children who work for the government. On weekends the population still empties to the farms to help parents or brothers or brothers-in-law with the seeding or the harvest or with the summer fallowing. Soft clerk's hands return to the wheel of a John Deere evoking memories from adolescence. Regina is a rural city. Its health and its economy swing precariously with that of the countryside beyond its city limits. Its people are rural people; hard-working, decent people. Generous people, but people with a strong sense of place and an acceptance of the way things are. Too rapid change is unsettling. Regina is a self-conscious city populated by self-conscious people. They are hurt by the sneers of neighbouring larger cities. They like to think that their town can cope with all exigencies. They like to think that their town can be a good place to live — for everybody.

There are Indians in Regina

On the way to my hotel, the taxi driver tells me that the Indians have just burned down two hotels in the area. As he explains it, "the hotel owners didn't mind, they were losing money and wanted to collect the insurance anyway. So they get 'em drunk and give 'em a few matches; nobody can prove a thing."

"The Indians in Regina are just the same as anybody else," the woman who tends bar in the hotel tells me. "I don't know why they're so defensive about it all the time. It's like they were paranoid."

Regina in the late 1970s was a very tense place. In 1977, for instance, there were five charges of police brutality awaiting disposition. All were levied by native people against the then all-white city police force. A skid-row bar was smashed to pieces. There was a stand-off between the Indians and the police. It was the wild west all over again. Some citizens described it as a totally lawless state with vigilante groups on both sides. The police were described as thugs out to harass the Indians who were increasingly visible in the centre of town. Some of the Indians were arming themselves with broken bottles and knives and sticks and were prepared to interpret the approach of any policeman as a hostile attack. Some people were comparing Regina to Kenora, Ontario, or an earlier Selma or Montgomery, Alabama. The merchants were distraught. An art store proprietor who had a shop downtown on Hamilton Street claimed that he couldn't get staff to work evenings. They were afraid to come downtown at night. On evenings when the store stayed open they would have to throw drunk Indians out. People in residential neighbourhoods worried about their safety and their property values. Calls were put out for a full-scale investigation.

Then the city fathers put the damper on. They got the leadership of the Indian organizations together and with the court system and the police force instituted the first race relations council of its kind in North America, the Regina Native Race Relations Association. They gave it a mandate to smooth the waters, investigate complaints immediately, educate both the Indians and the police about each other. In 1978 there were twenty-eight formal complaints by Indian people against the police force. By October 1979 there were only three. The city had relaxed.

But it remained on guard. The Svenson study for Indian Affairs on Indian and Métis issues in Saskatchewan to 2001 was entitled *The Explosive Years*. The introduction said:

The most important demographic trend in Saskatchewan for the next 25 years is the growth of the Indian ancestry population both in absolute terms and also as a proportion of the total population. This trend will have as large an impact on the nature of Saskatchewan as the rural-urban migration trends of the past fifty years. Given the present attitudes and policy orientations of non-Indians and judging from past experience in Indian-non-Indian relationships, the next 25 years could be years of racial turmoil in Saskatchewan. If racial turmoil does occur in Canada, it is likely to begin in Saskatchewan and spread to other areas. Major problems are likely to come to the surface first in Saskatchewan because of the relative size of the Indian ancestry population as compared to the total population and the rapidity with which the urbanization of the Indian ancestry population is occurring.

Svenson went on to describe the urban Indian population of Regina as young, with a higher proportion of females, while the on-reserve population tended to be male and older. He also discovered that a predominant part of the native population of Regina lived either in single-parent (female) families, or in multiple-family households. The number of both these types of families were far higher than the city average.

In Regina, says Ed Kempling, a United Church worker with that church's Native Concerns Committee, it all started with the revision of the Indian Act back in 1951. "The better health care," he says, "drastically cut the mortality rate of Indian people, particularly the infant mortality rate, without cutting the birth rate." Simultaneous changes in native education exposed Indian people to the larger society; they became aware of the country they were in and how they could be part of it. "Similarly," he points out, "nursing stations and schools encouraged permanent settlement; the transient hunter life ended and communities went on welfare."

The studies for Saskatchewan now assume that the growth rate for the total treaty Indian population will begin to rise as the relatively large number of children born in the years between 1959 and 1969 reach child-bearing age. This over-all growth rate will reach a peak in the late 1980s and will then decline again. It is also assumed that the on-reserve growth rates of recent years will not continue because the artificial direct job-creation activities of recent years will likely not be maintained at their present levels. So population growth will be off the reserves, in the cities.

There is no native ghetto in Regina, although the more cynical will call the entire city a ghetto. When you ask where the Indians live, people name neighbourhoods. Highland, Cathedral, North Central; mixed older neighbourhoods — not slums — rows of neat frame houses on small lots. Some of the housing is public, some not. Some is owned by native people.

One of the neighbourhoods, North Central, is close to the middle of the city. It is just across the tracks and north from downtown. A resident tells me that it was first settled by veterans of Middleton's army almost a century ago when they decided to stay on in the west after defeating Louis Riel and putting the Métis to rout. It is an old working-class neighbourhood with shaded streets because the trees have had a century to grow. The residents used to be totally Anglo-Saxon, now there is not a block that does not have at least one native family. Albert Elementary School in the centre of the neighbourhood has fifty per cent native enrolment. There has been some tension in North Central. One native couple who bought their house in 1971 say that it was a year before any of their neighbours would speak to them. A white resident explained that petitions occasionally are taken up to protest large native families moving onto a street. She explained it; "the old folks die and leave their homes to their children who live in the suburbs. The quickest way to make money is to rent the house through Social Services to an Indian family; the rent comes directly from welfare, there are no hassles. The tenants have no rights in this situation, the house doesn't get repaired, the neighbours get upset and blame the Indians. The neighbourhood becomes wary, especially if a couple of large Indian families move in."

Given the present situation with its minority citizens, the fact that Regina is a small city may be its blessing or its curse. It is too big to function in the ways small towns do where everyone takes his special social role. Though the role absorbs and freezes a person in its mould, there is a certain benevolence afforded by the fact that you are at least known as a person, with a name and a history. Small salvation, perhaps, from the ruthlessness that small town stigmatization can perpetuate, but salvation nonetheless. Yet Regina is not a city that is big enough to allow the anonymity that a huge city provides, alienating though that may be. Places as large as Toronto or New York provide a momentum that can sweep whole groups into their mix. This may not mean that the groups live better or happier lives, but the city itself has the capacity to absorb them and to function despite their presence. Even cities like Winnipeg or Edmonton have some of this capacity. Regina has it to a much lesser degree. That's why native people in Regina are noticed. That's why everyone in Regina has an opinion about them. That's why their presence and their projected presence has thrown the city into a flurry. That's why people on both sides are wary, either over-compensatory in their liberalism or overly brutal in their reaction.

In abstract ways people describe Regina as being a troubled city. Clement Blakeslee is a cultural anthropologist working in Winnipeg, His theory is that when a minority group gets to be twenty per cent or more of a city's population, trouble is at hand. "Ten per cent," he says, "a city can digest. Twenty per cent they can't." A minority group he defines as people who are viewed as outsiders and who are at the bottom of the heap. "They understand the definition and they react to it in a variety of ways, usually by raising hell. Consequently Regina is in deep bloody trouble."

Blakeslee says that the problems are never one way. The officialdom of the dominant group, he says, can hassle the subordinate group and the subordinate group reacts to the hassling by getting its back up. "It becomes a sort of waltz-step deterioration of relationships."

Ken Svenson believes that another way Regina is

challenged through its numbers of native people is economically, through the public financial commitments already made to social and support programs. He says that whereas in the past Indian people could only disrupt economic growth by taking a major initiative like going to war, now, with all the support programs already committed, Indian people as a group can significantly retard economic growth by doing nothing.

As a city, Regina faces some obvious challenges. Yet, in the old cliché, that makes Regina try harder. As will be seen in a subsequent chapter, Regina seems to have dealt very well with the potentially disastrous tensions between native people and the city's police force. The city, in that instance, had the guts to face the void squarely and find its way out. That may in the end make all the difference.

Edmonton

In Edmonton
- the police wear guns in open holsters.
- the bars and night spots all have dress codes that prevent people in jeans or even corduroys from coming in.
- the students have short hair and vote Conservative.
- the average income is $22,000 and poverty for a family of two is $8,000.
- the Jerry Lewis Telethon for Muscular Dystrophy nets $75,000, but the United Way scores close to the lowest per capita receipts in the country.
- men who have "made it" up north prowl into town in mud-splattered four-wheel drive Ram Chargers and Cherokee Chiefs and Broncos with bed rolls and survey equipment packed in the back.

- two hundred young men from Newfoundland and Quebec and Manitoba arrive every day in dilapidated cars or on Greyhound buses hoping to find the mother-lode. They get rooms at cheap hotels or live on watery soup at the men's hostels.
- the hookers on 105 and 106 streets paint their faces, put on high-heeled shoes, and are out working by three o'clock in the afternoon.
- young men wear big cowboy hats or look like they have just returned from the Klondike. Old men who have been to the Klondike shuffle around with scruffy whiskers, babbling to themselves.
- business men with pale blue eyes walk tall along Jasper Avenue discussing real estate and options and weaknesses in the Eskimos' defence.
- a former premier of the province is billed as the visiting Evangelist at a huge modern Pentecostal Auditorium just north of downtown.
- the present premier sits in his office plotting the mechanics of loaning some of the five billion dollars in the Heritage Fund to large corporations and deciding that, just for kicks, he might dangle a bit of it in front of the people of Quebec if they will decide not to separate from the Confederation.

Edmonton is different from other places in Canada. The difference is a little difficult to describe. Basically, it is called "boom". Edmonton feels like Dawson City must have felt eighty years ago. Edmonton looks like Houston. The feel is nervous energy, the kind of energy that makes people's knees bounce when they are sitting to talk to you. Or the kind of energy that makes them get up and walk around the room, still talking. All of Alberta, but particularly Edmonton, moves to a different energy, a different motivation than the rest of the country. Winnipeg worries about its declining population and its collective loss of nerve; Edmonton's population has increased by 250,000 in the last twenty years and promises to double in the next twenty, the city is eyeing an annexation of surrounding territory that will make it almost as big as Prince Edward Island. In Regina little neighbourhood groups encouraged by government bureaucrats are constantly having meetings to organize one thing or another to make their communities more co-operative, more neighbourly places; in Edmonton people are proud that they have made it on their own and refuse to understand how there could be any other way. In Toronto people talk almost to the point of religiosity about the conserver society, about how to live without throwing so many things away, taking it for granted that old buildings are to be refurbished, not razed; in Edmonton old buildings aren't razed one by one, downtown buildings are razed by the block and a movie crew doing an Alberta film has to travel to Winnipeg in order to find some still-existing period architecture to use for a backdrop. Dr. Schumacher's book, *Small Is Beautiful*, does not sell well in Edmonton.

Edmonton is the most future-looking of Canadian cities. Self confidence always presumes a future. Edmonton is awash in its own self confidence, like the high school valedictorian, brash and unabashedly self-assured. Cocky and gregarious. A combination, says one recent arrival from the United States, of Arizona politics and Bible belt.

Since 1966 Edmonton has grown from a quiet northern Alberta railway and agricultural town that always had possibilities, to a boom centre, controller of and gateway to the oil, gas, coal, and pipelines of northern Alberta and the Mackenzie Valley and a mecca for every hopeful luck chaser in the country.

From 1960 to 1980 the population of the city exploded from 350,000 to 600,000. A construction boom of unparalleled proportions ripped out and rebuilt the entire downtown creating a construction business worth over 700 million dollars in building permits in 1977 alone.

While the gas and oil continue to be found, while the pipelines continue to be proposed and built, and while the new systems to squeeze the tar-like heavy oil out of the muck continue to be perfected, Edmonton continues to grow and boom. That much is certain. But the keys to understanding the city lie somewhere else. They are hidden in a multitude of different currents and eddies.

A woman who works in the social services and who has lived in Edmonton all her life laments that "Edmonton is a city filled with people from somewhere else who have come to make money and only to make money. They have no other interest in the community."

Another woman who is a social planner and grew up elsewhere but has lived in Edmonton for a decade has decided that to understand Edmonton you need to understand how the Hudson's Bay Company works. In the beginning Edmonton was a Hudson's Bay Company town — Edmonton House — established in 1795. Everything grew from there. "Everything," she says, "is very proper, with the WASPS at the top. The other Anglo-Saxons run errands, the non-Anglo-Saxons do the joe jobs, and the Indians can come in through the back door but only if they have pelts with them." This is Edmonton's power structure. It all becomes somewhat complicated by the boom, but only physically. Who owns what and who calls the shots stays intact although the Ukrainians, she says, after decades in the city's north end, are starting to realize a little muscle.

There may be thirty to forty thousand Indians in Edmonton, between five and seven per cent of the population. No one knews for sure. All of Edmonton's populations shift rapidly, from day to day. At the Canadian Native Friendship Centre in the annex to an old red brick church on tree-shaded 117 Street there is a map of the city stuck full of little orange and yellow flags on pins. The orange flags are for status Indian families, the yellow for non-status or Métis families. The map is the result of a three-month survey undertaken by the centre early in 1979 and financed by the federal Department of the Secretary of State. As well as the map, there is a filing cabinet filled with one-page forms that list the names, numbers, ages, home community, and source of income for all the native families the survey managed to contact. On the map, the little flags are all over the place; south of the river and in the outlying suburbs as well as the thickest concentration — where there seems to be no room for another pin — in the centre of the city. But the map is incomplete. Whole neighbourhoods lie empty, barren, unpinned, deserted. The pile of white paper forms lies in the filing cabinet in disarray. The survey ran out of money and was never completed.

The people at the Canadian Native Friendship Centre say that if the Secretary of State gives more money, as they have been assured will be the case, the survey will be completed, the blank neighbourhoods on the map will get their pins and flags, the stacks of questionnaires will be compiled, and numbers, for a moment in time, will be frozen.

This is the way the native people's own organization has attempted to track down their people in the city. But beyond that, there is only a very vague sense of Indian people in Edmonton. Even though the numbers may be large, it is not like Regina or Winnipeg where the faces that go with the numbers are apparent. In Regina there is a significant consciousness of Indian people. In whatever form it takes, it stems from visibility, from encounters on the street, from newspaper stories, from the smallness of the city, from the speed at which things happen in the community. In Edmonton one has the feeling that everything is caught in the rush, that the passing cavalcade is a blur; that there is no time to notice anything. The Friendship Centre acknowledges that by the time they get the money to continue their survey, the rapidity with which things change in the city, the frequency with which people move, the transitory nature of everything, will have already made the work they have done redundant. Change in Edmonton bubbles like a hot sulphur spring, occasionally geysering, boiling over the top and shooting into the air, but always stirring, always bubbling, confounding anyone who would have it hold still if only for a moment.

Even the social planners have only vague helpless notions of things. A man at the Edmonton Social Planning Council says that he has no idea how many Indian people might be in Edmonton or how to find out. He says that he occasionally sees one on the street. He and the other people who work with him have genuinely no official and very limited private perspective on the native situation in Edmonton. The man I talk to is surprised by the population statistics I offer but is willing to speculate as to the reasons they have not come to the attention of the Social Planning Council. Are the numbers wrong? Not likely. Can it be that the natives, though significant in number, are adapting well and thus are not a social issue? Definitely not the experience of a couple of downtown social projects. Is the Social Planning Council not doing relevant work? Or are there so many things happening in Edmonton that the native situation just gets lost in the swirl? The latter is the most likely answer. Edmonton is a statistician's nightmare. Information is out of date before the ink on the report is dry.

Pat Murphy, who works at the city's Social Planning Division, says that her office would like to know more about the native people in the city but doesn't know where to start or where to fit it in with everything else. Services in the city can barely keep up with demands. There is a .05 per cent vacancy rate in housing. The Indians are just one more group who may or may not have an effect on the city. Nobody knows. The man at the Social Planning Council offers that if the city has a racial problem it is with East Indian people whose arrival has elicited a hostile and occasionally a violent reaction. With native people, no matter how rapidly they move in from the reserves or how quickly their numbers in the city grow, they are only one segment of a population that in total is growing and is projected to grow by over two thousand persons each month; East Indians, Maritimers, boat people, gold rush people from the four corners of the country and the world. The Indians are just one more group.

Not on Boyle Street they're not.

If Indian people are the invisible minority in Edmonton as a whole, in one little corner of the city, a patch of dilapidated blocks just east of downtown, they are a highly visible majority. The Boyle street area, 96 and 97 streets, is the city's skid row. Here, in the middle of Edmonton, in the centre of this city of boom and gold bathroom fixtures, are these streets of pawnbrokers and rundown hotels where eighty to ninety per cent of the people are native.

Why is this? What brings native people to the skids of the city? Why is the Indian view of the city so often from the bottom, looking up? Conversely, why is the city view of the Indian one that associates a whole people with the culture of skid row? That is where Indians in cities are most visible — so visible in fact that in western cities the Indian, with only scattered exceptions, possesses skid row.

One warm afternoon I sit pondering this in the New

Edmonton Hotel, in a bar room with faded green walls and cheap panelling decorated with old CN landscapes. The small round tables have blue terrycloth fitted tops; like shower caps over flat, hard-edged skulls. Two men are arguing in French at the next table. Across the aisle an old guy with straight grey hair is feeling up an Inuit girl who looks impassively at her beer. A poster on the wall explains that seventeen thousand drivers' licences were suspended in Alberta last year. Presumably this is to get people to cut back on their drinking, though that would be counter to the interests of the hotel. Perhaps the government makes them put up the poster. On the jukebox Hoyt Axton is singing that if you work your fingers to the bone you get bony fingers. A lot of bony fingers in this room. Not much fat of the land. No expense accounts.

The waitress calls me "luv" and has just evicted an old man named Swede from the next table because he was drunkenly threatening to fuck the two Indian girls sitting across from him. Behind me a guy with a black eye is arranging a party with a very fat woman and three eager young men.

There are ten hotels on "the row" in Edmonton. Hotels with tired old names like "The Royal", "The Empire", "The York" are strung out among the rooming houses, pawn shops, missions, and greasy spoon cafes. This is the Edmonton of Hugh Brody's classic study *Indians on Skid Row*. (Northern Science Research Group, DIAND, 1971) Perhaps Brody came closest to putting an understanding to the place of skid row in the life of the urban Indian. He wrote:

The skid row community is in many ways dominated by the Indians. They have evolved many of its norms and are easy within its ways. It is a world the migrant Indians understand. In these respects skid row is a unique corner of urban Canada. It stands between the limitations and constraints of a rural reserve and the rejection and alienation of white-dominated city life. The skid row area is a constant attraction to the migrant Indian. Just because it has a higher density of Indians it is likely that he will find friends there. Equally, if he has a job in a predominantly white and considerably prejudiced milieu, he can, whenever angry or frustrated, find consolation in the bars with fellow Indians. The Indians on skid row are always at pains to welcome newcomers from their own or any other reserve, and that makes skid row a natural terminal point for the urban migrant. And where skid row is the terminal point for the migrant, any attempts by Indian agencies, both provincial and federal to draw Indians into the main stream of Canadian life are likely to prove abortive.

Skid row dishes out life on the other side of the coin in every city; on Main Street in Winnipeg, down by the railway tracks in Regina. But in Edmonton it is life on the other side of the boom. The hustle and the flurry of everything else in Alberta has little relevance to the people who frequent the Boyle Street neighbourhood. It is like a bad joke.

The momentum that currently seizes Alberta is a mixed blessing. There are jobs and there is wealth, but there are enormous social costs and neither the time nor the perspective to deal with them. Since boom is a state of mind as much as it is anything else, it is built on hope. But the hopeless who luck out end up with the city having to look after them. In the late 1970s there were a thousand people a week arriving in Edmonton. An employment official said that for those with skills and trades there was work, good paying work, up north in the province and in the Northwest Territories. "But ninety per cent of the arrivals," he lamented, "had no skills, could get no jobs, and ended up staying on in the city." These were both whites and natives. And they came from all over the country. The prices they paid for their trouble were measured in frustration and anger. The price the city pays is measured in crime rates, social problems, and family break-ups.

In the boom it seems that there are at least as many casualties as there are winners. The social projects in the Boyle Street area pick up some of them. A smattering of social services pick up others. I visited one afternoon at a house in the north end of the city where a Canada Employment Service-sponsored project attempts to help Indian women who have been on welfare prepare themselves for jobs. Each session takes ten women and lasts seven weeks. The course teaches them how to dress, how to groom themselves, how to fill out forms, how to approach an employer, how to cope with their children while they are working. The project coddles the women along through practice (work experience) jobs. Then it sends them out on their own. One out of three makes it.

There are enormous ironies in Edmonton's story. One social worker commented that while the image of Edmonton is that of a rich city and the truth is that many individuals are very well off, Edmonton is possibly the worst city in the country in which to be poor. The richer the place, the maxim seems to go, the less tolerance, time, concern, or even notion it has of and for poverty. While not all the Indians in Edmonton are as deeply sunk in material poverty as the people on Boyle Street, neither are they, by any stretch, wealthy.

Winnipeg
Indian Days

It happens every summer now, on a vacant city block in downtown Winnipeg. A stage and booths and a big tent for dancing all appear like magic as do a row of tipis squatting like Buddhas with the skyscrapers of downtown towering behind them. Indian Days. For three days and nights they roll in in cars and vans and pickup trucks; on Greyhound buses and by thumb from all over Manitoba, southern Saskatchewan, northwest Ontario, and from scattered reservations in Minnesota and North Dakota. The people come in from the suburbs, up from Main Street, down from the tenements and rooms that stretch back into the crowded neighbourhoods that surround this vacant block. And for three days they gather and sing and dance and eat and sit around until the grass is trampled and brown on this, the hottest weekend of July.

The crowd chatters in Cree and Saulteaux, Assiniboine, Sioux, Ojibway. Men in cowboy boots, babies in strollers. Curly-haired people with dark eyes and French names. Stern-looking young men wearing Red Power buttons; smooth-skinned young girls with lustrous black braided hair stuck with eagle feathers, wearing brilliant, beautiful satin and beaded costumes for the pow wow dancing; a grinning scruffy-haired man holding a bottle of beer and wearing a T-shirt which proclaims, "It's Fun To Be Canadian". Two old men in white shirts and baseball caps separately pull me aside to whisper earnestly, "See what Indians can do when you let them?"

The pow wow dancing goes on all day and into the night under the big tent, its walls rolled up and tied to let the breeze and the light filter in. Tribe after tribe enters the tent through the beauty of its young; children blossoming to adulthood dressed in skins and silks and beads and feathers and shuffling flat-footed to the primeval rhythms of the drums and the wailing cries of the singers as they elicit some vague notion of the sensibilities of their ancestors.

Outside, past the greasy smells of hamburgers and frying bannock, past old grandmothers smiling over infants asleep in their arms, is the stage where the ultimate synthesis locks into place; a tall lean young Indian in a rakishly tilted cowboy hat singing Tom T. Hall songs. Cowboy music. The country-singing contest is won by a busty white girl who belts out Jeannie Pruett's "Satin sheets to lie on, satin pillows to cry-hi-hi on. . . ." The crowd howls its approval.

As the fiddles scream and the jigging contests start, the Lieutenant-Governor of Manitoba wanders alone around the edge of the fair, in his shirt sleeves, smoking a cigarette.

Beyond, in the hotels and bars and tall office buildings, the business of Winnipeg goes on.

In October of 1978 the papers in Winnipeg carried stories about the problems of the city core and of the population shift that was taking place from the inner city to the suburbs. Under a headline "Inner City Dying as People Leave", the *Winnipeg Tribune* quoted a report prepared as part of the city's development planning that cited: a 38 per cent decline in population in Winnipeg's core between 1941 and 1976; a 180 per cent population increase in the suburbs during the same period; a large stock of older, poor quality housing, primarily in the inner city, with few signs of rejuvenation; and social and racial problems resulting from the large, steady influx of native Indians into the core area.

Within a week, city Indian leaders were condemning the report for blaming Indian people for the decline of the inner city and for painting native people as "poverty-stricken drunkards and prosti-

tutes". The report hadn't painted native people as poverty-stricken drunkards and prostitutes. But it had suggested, as the *Winnipeg Tribune* reported it, that:

> The most visible social problem in the Inner City, and particularly the core area, is the Indian problem. Between 1961 and 1971 the Indian population grew nearly 500 percent, and almost all the newcomers moved into the core area. Each year roughly 1,000 more Indians migrate to Winnipeg. Federal cutbacks on immigration from other countries will have a marked effect on Winnipeg, and could well make the native influx the largest migration coming into the city. This native migration and the problems it causes must be "addressed very seriously". Because these people are usually low income and relatively transient they occupy the worst housing in the Inner City and create a need to keep this housing on the market. Racial problems also arise as homeowners react with alarm at a perceived influx of Indians into their neighborhood. There is a perception that following the American experience, an influx of native persons into an area is an indication of the final stages of deterioration of the area.

Indian leaders were incensed. In reacting, the head of the Winnipeg Indian Council was quoted as saying; "It is offensive to suggest all our people are poor." The president of the Indian and Métis Friendship Centre called a press conference and told reporters, "The tone of the report suggests the area's Indian population is to blame for the Inner City's problems. After reading it, my reaction is one of great indignation and disgust."

Neither the report nor the media's reporting of it really blamed native people for the condition of the city core. More blame by far was laid at the feet of forty years of politicians' and developers' decisions. Nor did the report go to lengths to explain that large numbers of native people live as well in the suburbs and are active contributing members to the city's economy and society. But that wasn't its purpose. Its purpose was to describe what Winnipeg looked like in the late 1970s, and to identify some of the issues the city would have to look at in order to survive with any degree of vitality and health.

What the reactions of the native leaders indicate is how sensitive and close to the surface issues of race are in Winnipeg.

Estimates of the number of native people living in Winnipeg range from a low of twenty-five thousand to highs of sixty and eighty thousand. Generally accepted numbers hover around the forty to sixty thousand mark or just slightly less than ten per cent of the city's six hundred thousand population. As is the case in other centres, numbers are hard to come by and can never be precise. They are estimates, or better "guesstimates".

The 1971 census indicated that there were at that time 6,420 persons in Winnipeg who traced an Indian ancestry through the father's line. Census data concerning native people is generally considered to be under-estimated because the census is unable to count (and therefore doesn't include) itinerant new arrivals. Other ways of making estimates in Manitoba are to take numbers of status Indian people from the Department of Indian Affairs and multiply by three in order to accommodate non-status and Métis people for a total for native people. Another way is to take the known number of school children in a particular group and multiply by four to obtain an estimate for the total population of that group. Chancy estimates, but this is the sort of arithmetic that is used to obtain the forty-to-sixty thousand figures. What is known more precisely, and what is perhaps more important than absolute numbers, is trends. And what is known and often quoted in Winnipeg is that the number of native people in that city increased nearly five hundred per cent between 1961 and 1971. That is a trend that for various reasons was anticipated to continue, and prompted one observer, social anthropologist Clement Blakeslee, to speculate in a well publicized paper for the provincial cabinet, that by 1985 the native population of Winnipeg could reach a hundred thousand persons. *

The migration, Blakeslee said, comes not only from Manitoba but from Saskatchewan and northwestern Ontario. He predicted a continuing rural-urban migration for a few years combined with a substantial spurt in the "born in Winnipeg" native population. He wrote; "Roughly 50% of the status Indians are less than fifteen years old. Therefore, the family formation rate in the coming decade will be staggering."

The various media have kept the presence of native people in Winnipeg a high profile issue. So it could be that native leaders like the ones who took issue with the urban-core stories have reason to be sensitive. Periodically dramatic stories slip into the city's media of Indian people, fresh to the city, living six or seven to an eight-by-ten foot hovel down on the riverbank and saying things like; "We prefer the riverbank to the city's slum housing," or "It's just like being back on the reserve." There is no shortage of material that can serve both to point out the inadequacies of the city and to raise fear and tension levels in both white and native communities.

But it seems that it is not all done gratuitously. Some people are definitely worried about issues raised by the influx of large numbers of native people, and about Winnipeg's capacity to cope with

*The Secretary's Interim Report to the Inter-Governmental Relations Sub-Committee of Cabinet and Indian Services Committee, March 1976

those issues. Alan Howison, the director of one of the city's major charitable foundations says that coming to terms with the issues between native people and the city will be Winnipeg's major challenge in the 1980s. He feels that integrating the native people into the fabric of the city is mandatory in order for the city to survive and flourish, and he worries about the two things which make this difficult; a low self-image on the part of native people as a group, and an equally troubling low image of native people held by the white community.

Jim Cartlidge, the president of the city's Chamber of Commerce, is concerned enough that he has held discussions with an inner-city social agency where Indian teenagers pass a proportion of their time and has directed a Chamber committee to come up with wide-ranging suggestions to enable the entire membership to hire more young Indian people. He adds, "If we're going to deal with this problem we're prepared to acknowledge that we may have to allow for some major dislocations."

Cyril Keeper, a former city councillor, now a member of parliament, and a native, acknowledges that the racial tensions in Winnipeg are disturbing. "When I was campaigning for an inner-city ward," he says, "I became aware of the hostility that exists in downtown Winnipeg toward native people." Keeper believes that the tensions arise from white people who live in the downtown area coming into contact with native people who live troubled lives. And this, rightly or wrongly, creates and reinforces stereotypes. Large numbers, admits Keeper, appear threatening. And the more fear and threat there is, the more potential for conflict.

Winnipeg has always been an interesting city because of the inappropriateness of all its mixes. Ideally, it should look like Regina, a much smaller, more one-dimensional distribution centre servicing a very definite agricultural hinterland. But Winnipeg is not like that at all. From the beginning it had a sense of itself as a world-class crossroads. In its heyday (perhaps 1890–1920) it was referred to as "the Chicago of the north" and it filled itself with gems of Chicago-inspired beaux arts architecture. Winnipeg was the capital of the west and until very recently remained the major city of western Canada. The grain barons who lived along Wellington Crescent were as influential during the first three decades of this century as any industrialist the country has produced. Winnipeg was never a rural city filled with men and women who didn't want to farm any longer. From the beginning it mixed British, French, and a delicatessen of eastern Europeans into a rich and varied and very urban culture.

Winnipeg is unlike Edmonton as well. It may have had a boom, but it can't remember it. Winnipeg worries instead about its decline. Planners and social scientists roll out report after report of falling populations, of predictions for slow or negative economic growth. Real estate prices are among the lowest in the country. People who live by expanding populations and expanding economies gnash their teeth. Winnipeg is a dry town for a fast-buck artist. The civic mood in the late 1970s came perilously close to a severe crisis of spirit. Winnipeg watched as it sons and daughters moved to Toronto, and then to Alberta. Both of Manitoba's prevailing ideologies, small "s" socialist and small "c" conservative, were blamed in turn for what was essentially the result of an accident of geography; the fact that Winnipeg wasn't, like its younger sisters to the west, head over heels in a frantic whirlwind courtship with a wealthy destiny.

In the long run, both of these things may turn out to be Winnipeg's strengths and perhaps its salvation. Winnipeg has always been able to muster determination and creativity when it needed it. And no one group of its citizens has ever held a unique corner on this ability. Winnipeggers are at long last beginning to appreciate and celebrate the fact that the first independent government in the west was born on the banks of the Red River — when one Louis Riel proclaimed a provisional government at Fort Garry in 1869. Creative and daring solutions to the problems and burdens of geography, politics, and isolation didn't stop there. Among other things, Winnipeg spent its first century taming a flood-prone Red River by building one of the biggest ditches in the world; amalgamating twelve disparate municipalities into one city; and creating and promoting a world-class ballet company.

Nor has creativity been lacking in the native community. When the Friendship Centre movement got under way in Canada in the early 1960s, Winnipeg's centre was a pioneer, providing the energy and the talent for many other centres throughout the country. Today it remains one of the largest. And though Neeginan (see chapter five) was never built, it was in Winnipeg that the imagination was sparked to design this astonishing concept for an urban Indian village.

In many quarters the panic over Winnipeg's slow growth or no growth seems to be subsiding. Indeed there are a collection of thinkers who argue increasingly that slower is better and that that is the best card in the city's hand at the present time. Even the president of the Chamber of Commerce, an organization that is usually affiliated genetically with the growth syndrome, can say that he sees the city's future as "bright, if not flamboyant".

In spite of problems, Winnipeggers have a depth of commitment to their city that inspires a high degree of municipal involvement. For example, even though the city ranks eightieth in the country in per capita income, its citizens are perennially among the most generous in giving to the United Way. This commitment, combined with the time slow growth allows, will see the city through a host of problems, one would like to think, including the tough ones of adjustment to its population of native people.

Tim Sale, the executive director of the city's Social Planning Council, a research and support body to the city's social services, sees most of the problems Winnipeg is encountering which involve native people as the problems of poverty, and the problems engendered by a group suffering from poverty. The most hopeful thing he sees at the moment is that the slowing that is occurring in Winnipeg will allow the city in the end to absorb a poverty group, this poverty group, into its work force.

Doreen Wyatt, Regina

Doreen Wyatt is Métis and comes from a family that has lived in Regina for over twenty years. She is married to a white and is entering her fourth year of psychology at the University of Regina. Tall and chic and ambitious, she tells me how her father wanted to be white and didn't teach his children (thirteen through two marriages) any Indian language. She also tells me how they avoided the family of an uncle who "drank a lot" and thus was at odds with the image their family wanted to create for itself. Doreen was the first in her family to go to university. She laments her lack of knowledge of her heritage and says this summer she is going to northern Saskatchewan to the reserve where her mother (now dead) was born and where an uncle still lives to see what she can find out about her roots.

When her father moved to the city, she says, people felt obliged to hide the fact that they were native. Now it is more acceptable if not, in some circles, "in", but for people like her it may be too late. They have lost too much over the years by trying to hide it.

I remember going back up north on a few occasions, but I don't remember our life before we moved to the city; I was only one or two. We didn't learn any native language as children. I imagine my parents made a decision not to teach us any Cree or Saulteaux figuring that if English is the language that we have to use, then that is what we would have to be taught. I remember other people speaking Cree and Saulteaux in the house, but we weren't allowed to learn it. I just picked up a few words. When people came to visit from up north, I couldn't understand what they were saying. And when the children didn't speak any English at all,

it was very difficult to find out what they wanted. They'd get mad at us and we'd get mad at them. . . . My father is a very authoritarian sort of person, you know, I guess he didn't figure we needed to know about any of these things. Especially not the five girls. But I've been asking a lot of questions in the last few years. I would get my stepmother to ask my father about things so that she could then tell me.

I've decided that this summer I'm going to go up north and find my roots. I guess the best bet is to go to the reserves and ask around and see if people remember. I need to do it now because five or ten years from now might be too late, I'm relying on old peoples' stories and what they remember. I'm going to try to find my godmother and talk to her. I can't remember her at all. I hope she is still alive.

I never knew I was Indian until I was in grade five and someone mentioned it to me. We lived around all white people. It was really a shock. We tried to ignore it. People usually thought we just had lovely dark skin! Later I found myself more open, maybe that's why now I want to find out more of these things. I relate to the other native people in the city now. More than I did when I was growing up. I think it's in the last three years since I have started to actively identify myself as a native. It probably started when I went to university and opened up my perspective, opened up to other things than just myself.

Up until that time we never "passed for whites"; some people are so fair that they do pass for white. It was just all our goals and values, you know, saving your money, getting a better education, getting a good job, all these things. These were the ways we were taught to think, these were our values. Those were the goals the society around us set for people.

Lots of times I did encounter various types of discrimination — people calling you an Indian, or not talking to you, snubbing you, especially in the stores. Just petty little things, nothing outright. I'll always remember one little boy who was always a mean little kid, oh I hated his guts. He was always teasing us, pulling our hair, calling us names. But it's only ignorant people who do that; they don't know any better. So I don't pay any attention to it when someone says something. What's the point in it?

It's hard, though, for some people to handle that. We had a ball tournament last summer and the Bluebells, the girls' team from the Friendship Centre, were playing in it. Just as the game was almost over, someone from the crowd, this was a mixed crowd, said something derogatory to the girls, God knows what. Anyway our coach got very mad, ran over and slugged the guy. And the Bluebells got thrown out of the tournament. Because some stupid fool in the crowd opens his big mouth to say something sick.

You want to hear scary stories? Regina is really bad about that sort of thing, prejudice. Real subtle. The ones who are open about it are probably more honest than the ones who pretend that "Indian people are okay."

During the next few years the things that will be important to native people in Regina are housing, education, and jobs. The same basic things. If any group has those things they are more important than worrying about prejudice and native organizations. Satisfy their basic needs and then they can use their free time and devote it to doing good works and things like that. The things that are important to achieving identity in the city have to do with the way you are brought up, with developing and keeping your values. I think that's how you get an identity. It's something you are brought up with, surrounded by. Since I missed that, I've now got to make my identity, so to speak. Where do you go? What I'm doing now, working, reading, going to conferences of my people, trying to find out what's going on. I won't say I have got it yet, maybe I never will have it. But you have to keep trying.

City Issues

In their book *Indians without Tipis*, Bruce Sealey and Verna Kirkness write:

> Native people estimate that perhaps 15-20% of those migrating to the city encounter serious problems; possibly 30-35% encounter some problems but receive help from Friendship Centres or various social agencies and ultimately become adjusted to city life. The other 50% experience few difficulties and, other than having the problem of retaining their Indian culture, are successful and relatively happy in the city. Those who fail form a dejected minority who comprise a hard core of "Main Street" (skid row) types. These reinforce the stereotypes held of Indians by so many whites.

Some things, like education and hopes for schools that both reflect and are concerned about native history and experience, are the concerns of all native people in the city. But other matters — adequate housing, employment and income for those with few job skills and thin job histories, police and law enforcement issues — are rarely the preoccupation of the successful fifty per cent of urban migrants. These things might all be termed "poverty issues", matters that more often affect poor people. Ask any social worker, planner, administrator, policeman, educator, counsellor, politician. Ask any native spokesperson. These are areas where native people, particularly those who are poor or unsophisticated in the ways of urban society, have difficulties, sometimes severe difficulties. And the cities, in turn, believe that it is the arrival of native people which causes concern and difficulties. Problems are identified which become the subjects of on-going public dialogue. Phalanxes of workers are dispatched to talk about and deal with the issues. The issues are at the root of discussions about expenditures of money and energy. They are the sore points on the communal body.

The issues are enormously difficult both for native people and for the cities. While they involve private passions and private fears, they are essentially public or group issues. They centre around the ways one group, the urban community as it existed prior to the arrival of native people, interacts with another group, the native people who are moving to the cities. They spring frequently from a vast gap in understanding and communication. And, as often, they spring from a desire by the city to accommodate native people (or any immigrating people for that matter) on the city's own terms, only to find out that that is not entirely possible.

Housing

Housing is rarely a problem for rich people, rich native people included. So when housing becomes an issue that faces the native in the city, the implication is that what is being talked about is not really housing, but poverty. The quality, the adequacy, and the very availability of housing becomes a day-to-day issue for many urban natives because many native people, a disproportionate number of native people, are also poor. Some are despondently poor.

The Indian and Métis Friendship Centre in Winnipeg is a low, rambling complex at the end of a narrow street in what is known as Winnipeg's core. Not far to the east and south are the tall shadows of downtown office buildings and hotels. Surrounding the Friendship Centre is a city core community consisting of rows of houses across streets from fruit company warehouses and backed by cookie factories. Laced through the community are playgrounds in vacant lots and on construction sites; sporadic highrises built for old folks; schools with smudged windows and hard-packed, beaten, trampled playgrounds; stubby and well-climbed trees; corner grocery stores with thick plywood shutters that lock nightly over the front windows; and back lanes littered with broken bottles where winos have partied.

The rows of wooden houses stand side by side like relatives, each of whom has seen a different fortune. A house shuttered and boarded with drifts of broken glass in the yard stands next to a brightly painted dwelling with not a weed on the lawn and a plastic-flower-filled planter running the length of the lace-curtained front window. Next to these is a row of new public housing built in trendy geometric shapes but all painted the same, and then the charred shell of a dwelling where a grandmother and two infants perished one winter's night when the ancient furnace blew up.

Don Marks is a community worker at the Friendship Centre. He surveys the neighbourhood. He explains that the Friendship Centre has three full-time housing counsellors who do nothing but take people around trying to help them find a decent place to live. Friendship Centre representatives are continually trekking back and forth to city hall to lobby for more and better housing. He points to a new three-storey apartment building, a half a block long, that the Friendship Centre is hoping to manage on behalf of the Manitoba provincial housing corporation and where they will give priority to native tenants. He says this part of the city is an area where a lot of native people live and where a lot of native people settle when they come to the city. "Natives," says Marks, "don't want to live in the suburbs, but downtown where their friends and family are and where the jobs are." Then he talks about a survey that shows that of 330 older (over forty) native persons living in the area, twenty-three per cent were paying over sixty per cent of their incomes for housing and forty per cent were paying over fifty per cent. He complains about the policies of the provincial public housing authority, who, he says, will use a two-month waiting list for their suburban town-houses to beg off building more dwellings in the inner city where the waiting list is two years long. And he tells of people who move into Winnipeg from the reserves and rural communities and have no idea what they should get for the money they are paying. "They are people," he says, "who will pay $225 for a dive and be impressed because it has a toilet."

Marks summarizes the housing problems for native people who are poor but are trying to make it in the city — if you are poor you take what you can get; you forfeit your right to complain; and you still pay, relative to what other people pay, a large share of your income for your shelter. If you are unsophisticated in the ways of the city or if you have trouble with language or if you have any of a myriad of other disadvantages, you are in double jeopardy. An Urban Housing Survey published by the Manitoba Indian Brotherhood in 1971 starts out with these words:

It soon becomes apparent to the Indian new-comer that his problems have not been left behind him but in fact have relocated with him, although now they are more subtly manifested.

Upon arrival in the city — usually with the most meager of personal possessions and minimal financial resources, the Indian's primary concern is in locating accommodation. If he is alone, his chances are markedly improved. If, however, as in a considerable number of instances, he is encumbered with a wife and several children, his potentialities are infinitely reduced.

If he is fortunate enough to have friends or relatives residing in the city, he may obtain temporary lodging for his family in an already over-crowded, generally substandard dwelling in some deteriorating section of the city's inner core. . . . We contend that the chain of circumstance by which the newly-arrived Indian is confronted often irrevocably shackles him to an existence of hopelessness and degradation. We further contend that the first link in this blighted chain of events is forged by the type of accommodation into which he is thrust.

We submit that the Indian has consistently occupied the lowest level of housing in the city, to the extent that one could consider such accommodation the private preserve of the native populace.

A report prepared in 1975 for Neeginan Manitoba Inc. about conditions for native people in Winnipeg states at one point:

As might be expected, the native families residing in the core are to be found in the cheapest and worst dwellings that have been left behind by their former occupants whose circumstances have improved sufficiently to permit them to move into better housing elsewhere in the city. It is interesting to note that there is not as yet a concentration of native residents in any one area. The pattern here is not one based on the ethnic enclave or continuous racial slum. Rather it is a pattern based on the random scattered location of the slum dwellings.

A number of studies have been undertaken that include assessments of housing and how it affects native people in Winnipeg. They include the report prepared for Neeginan Manitoba by the consulting firm of Damas and Smith (1975); *Winnipeg's Core Area, an Assessment of Conditions Affecting Law Enforcement* prepared by the Institute of Urban Studies at the University of Winnipeg (1975); and *Plan Winnipeg*, a report to the Winnipeg Tri-Level Committee on Urban Affairs from the Winnipeg Development Plan Review (1978).

On the basis of census data and other information the studies take for granted that at least half of Winnipeg's forty to sixty thousand native people, or twenty-five thousand persons, live in the downtown core of the city. This is almost a third of the total downtown population.

The same surveys describe the characteristics of core-area housing in Winnipeg. The Plan Winnipeg report described inner-city housing in the following categories: four per cent very poor; nineteen per cent poor; sixty-eight per cent fair; and only nine per cent good. According to the same report, eighty-five per cent of the housing stock in the core was constructed prior to 1946, seventy per cent was constructed prior to 1920, and a mere ten per cent after 1960. According to the University of Winnipeg survey, "there is a high incidence of absentee ownership in the core. Rates of tenant occupancy to owner occupancy are 3-1. The rate of tenancy exceeds that of the outer city by forty per cent."

The deterioration of housing has been compounded by a net population shift away from the core of the city over the past forty years. From 1941–1976 the population of the core area of Winnipeg dropped by thirty-eight per cent from 128,212 to 79,334. So there were not the population pressures that would motivate either the private or the public sector to upgrade, repair, or replace deteriorating housing stock. In fact the opposite occurred; housing was allowed to deteriorate until it was beyond repair and then it was demolished. Its only reprieve would be to be allowed to stand empty, beyond habitation, an eyesore and a firetrap, for a few years before demolition. But inevitably it was demolished and rarely was it replaced. Between 1972 and 1976 forty-eight per cent of residential demolitions in Winnipeg were in the core area. In the same years the core only accounted for six per cent of new housing starts. There was no reason to build new housing or repair the old — people were leaving. Winnipeg's suburban population between 1941 and 1976 increased by 180 per cent. Everybody was moving away from downtown. Everybody, that is, except native people.

Native people were moving *in*. Their inheritance was this collection of old and deteriorating housing that nobody else wanted anymore and that nobody much wanted to upgrade or replace. And yet, with a city-wide apartment vacancy rate in 1977 at just over one per cent, there was not a lot of choice. People were lucky to get a place even if it was only fair or poor or very poor. Nor did they get a break economically. The Plan Winnipeg survey shows Winnipeg to be among the most expensive cities in the country with regard to the proportion of income tenants pay for housing. In Winnipeg thirty-seven per cent of renting households pay more than twenty-five per cent of their incomes for housing and seventeen per cent pay more than forty per cent. Don Marks claims that some native people in the neighbourhood around the Friendship Centre paid an even higher percentage. And, as he also points out, many native people, new to the city are at a severe disadvantage in assessing the value of what they are in fact paying for.

Neeginan: The Village That Never Was

It would have been somewhere along the river, probably nestled in behind the conglomeration of "culture centres" — Concert Hall, Theatre Centre, Planetarium, Museum — that inhabit two or three redeveloped city blocks on the east side of Main Street. It would have been tucked away in the shadow of the rising ramp of the expressway that bleeds out of the downtown, over the river and the tracks and into the northern suburbs. It would have been a walk from Main Street, from the hotels and cafes that form the so-called "drag", and it would have been neighboured by warehouses and aging factories. Just to the south would have loomed the towers of the business heart of the city at Portage and Main. That's where it would have been, if it had been built.

Depending on who one talks to, Neeginan would have been either the boldest attempt ever made by a city, certainly in Canada, to encompass the needs and aspirations of a portion of its populace, or it would have been a monstrous failure, a monument built to segregation and the solidifying of the status quo at the expense of anything human and volatile and changing. Neeginan was envisaged as an "Indian village in the middle of downtown Winnipeg" replete with schools, arts and cultural facilities, shopping, headquarters for political and cultural organizations, and facilities for health and social services. As the report on the feasibility study put it:

> Whatever scheme is formulated, it seems that basic to it must be the preservation of the group. This is a common need amongst people who find themselves in a strange and hostile environment. It can be observed amongst immigrants from abroad who gravitate to the same few blocks in their new city, so that they can be with their own

people. "Little Italy" and "Chinatown" are two of the innumerable examples of such ethnic enclaves. Indeed, this is the reason for the strength of the reserves, and the reason why the Indians objected so violently to the federal government's recent proposal to dissolve them. The reserve represents the only security that the Indian knows; it is the only place in the world where he feels at home and where he can be with his own people on his own terms. It was recognition of the need for this kind of community which lay behind Kahn-Tneta Horn's proposal that a new reserve be built outside of Winnipeg as a solution to the problem of that city's Indian population. Some kind of special community is probably a basic requirement in any scheme which may be devised. Only instead of being outside the city, it should be within the city, at or near the place where the Indians are now concentrated. And instead of being a reserve, it should be an ethnic quarter not unlike the other ethnic quarters in this and other cities. It should have its own schools and its own stores and its own clinics. And it should be designed and built with the advice and participation of the Indians themselves.

Neeginan had auspicious beginnings. The idea was pushed early by, among others, the then director of the Indian and Métis Friendship Centre, George Munroe, and by the then Director of Planning for the city of Winnipeg, Earl Levin. These two, with the assistance of a handful of others, were able to garner support both from the native community and from various agencies of government. Ultimately a corporation was formed called "Neeginan Manitoba Inc.", *Neeginan* being a Cree word which translates to mean "our place". The corporation was chartered in early 1973 and by late 1973 had entered into agreement with the federal government to undertake a feasibility study around the urban village concept. The study was to be carried out for the corporation by a Winnipeg consulting firm called Damas and Smith Limited, and the findings were to be made available to a unique multi-governmental agency known as the tri-level committee. The tri-level committee encompassed representatives of the city of Winnipeg, the provincial ministry of urban affairs, and the federal minister of state for urban affairs. The terms of reference for the feasibility study were to explore what such a village ought to be like, investigate how housing would be a part of it, provide information for the choice of a site, and provide the nitty gritty information on matters like procedures for land acquisition, cost, anticipated problems, the design and function of a large service centre that would form the focal point of the village, and so on.

Most interesting were the objectives of the Neeginan corporation, objectives they hoped would be given form by the feasibility study and later by the actual construction of the "village". These were:

1. To provide a decent place for the urban Indian to live in the city where he can be with his own people, speak his own language, follow his own customs, and enjoy the supports and strengths inherent in this type of ethnic community, much as he does on the reserve but in an urban context.

2. To act as a reception and orientation centre for the Indian coming to Winnipeg from the reserve where he can find enough which is familiar to him so that he can make the adjustment to city life in his own time and his own way.

3. To provide contacts with the city so that life in the Indian community is not a closed ghetto but is open-ended, so that movement back and forth between the city and the Indian community is made easy.

4. To provide facilities for education in his own language, training, personal development, the development of managerial and entrepreneurial skills. . . . There should be sought out the genuinely talented in the community who can develop as real painters, musicians, sculptors, poets, actors, dancers, and a place should be provided for them to bring their art to the community at large.

5. To provide an urban preserve for the cross-cultural enrichment of all citizens.

Neeginan Report

The feasibility study went on for a little over a year (between February 1974 and April 1975) at a cost — mostly to the federal government — of $78,000. Meetings were held, surveys were attempted, questionnaires were distributed, specialists were consulted. Ultimately, four sites just to the north of Winnipeg's downtown business core were investigated. The sites ranged from 11.6 to 26.7 acres and each was checked out as to ease and cost of acquisition, preference by native organizations and various native individuals, proximity to existing facilities and services, and proximity to the Red River (the desire to incorporate the west bank of the Red River into the community remained consistent in the planners' minds throughout).

Early drawings were made of an elaborate Community Services Centre that was to be the focal point for the village and was to incorporate almost everything from shops to schools to the offices of social agencies and political organizations, as well as some housing for old folks and transients.

Projections about land acquisition and construction costs for this services centre building ran in the five-million-dollar range.

In April of 1975 the report of the feasibility study for Neeginan was issued in a full-colour seventy-two-page book. Then — nothing happened.

Actually many things happened, but nothing that would move Neeginan, the Indian village in the middle of the urban jungle of Winnipeg, from being a plan in a book to being a reality. Though accounts of what happened after the feasibility study report was presented vary from person to person and are wrapped with a sort of perplexing confusion, two reasons for the project's demise seem to emerge. The various governments who would have had to pay for it all were frightened off by size and cost. And the Indian leadership in Winnipeg, who would have had to push the project vigorously in order to have it proceed, lost steam. The report on the feasibility study was presented in a flurry of optimism. And while it seems that no one at any given point actually said "No", that it could not proceed; neither did anyone say "Yes". Various levels of government did nothing to encourage the pursuance of the project; George Munroe left the Friendship Centre and the Indian leadership dissipated; the Neeginan board of directors continued for some time, awaiting a mandate from someone to continue, and then it too disbanded. By 1977 Neeginan was dead.

The Neeginan idea was interesting both for its uniqueness and its boldness. It was criticized for proposing the creation of a ghetto, but rarely, anywhere, had anyone ever set out deliberately to create a ghetto like this one, and been prepared to defend its merits.

Earl Levin, the city planner, still argues vehemently for his "ghetto model":

Neeginan assumed that the condition of the urban native is analogous to the situation of the European immigrant except that the Indians do not have the advantage of the ghetto. The ghetto can provide an incubator and an environment of language, people, and support with which he is familiar. Given the eastern European and Jewish communities in north Winnipeg, it would have been in the best tradition of Winnipeg social organization. But the Indian instead comes to Winnipeg and bleeds to death on the sidewalk in front of a Main Street hotel.

Levin likes to add with as much irony as he can muster that "nobody ever seemed to worry whether or not the reservations might be ghettos."

Others are prepared to argue with as much vehemence against Levin's position. Ed Letinsky, another Winnipeg planner, says that the various governments made the right decision by refusing to pour large amounts of money into a "monument". The governments, he says, "by concentrating the dollars on programs instead, kept their priorities in line. Besides, by this time the native people were fearing that a project of this scale would have been taken completely out of their hands and run instead by a bunch of white bureaucrats." Other critics were as forceful and as scornful, again raising points about expensive concrete monuments and ghettos that, rather than fostering a group's identity, solidify it and then prevent interaction with the other parts of the society. But in the middle if it all was a third group who were profoundly disappointed.

Stanley McKay is Cree. In his mid-sixties, he has been in Winnipeg since 1959. By the time he was asked to sit on the board of directors of Neeginan Inc., he had been both chairman of the Winnipeg Indian Council and the director of a hostel run by the United Church for transient native people.

Stanley McKay is disappointed that Neeginan

did not happen both because of the amount of work he and others did between 1973 and 1976, and because of the things he wanted in the city that he feels Neeginan could have provided. He says that he would like to have seen services for native people centralized in a complex like Neeginan. "The problem," he says, "is still the runaround that people, especially people who are in need, get from one agency to another, from one organization to another." He also says, from his experience at the United Church reception lodge and at the Friendship Centre, some residences were needed, "a few houses for newcomers where they could live until they were oriented to the city." This, in his mind, Neeginan ought to have provided.

McKay is upset about the runaround the Neeginan board got when they started making their approaches to various government agencies for capital to get the project going once the feasibility study was done. Part of this he blames on an abandonment of city people by the one government department that looks after Indian people everywhere else — the Department of Indian and Northern Affairs. They would not look at Neeginan. The federal government's representative in the discussions was, instead, the ministry of state for urban affairs. Says McKay, "This is one of the problems we have as Indians in the city; that though we are recognized by the Manitoba Indian Brotherhood [the Winnipeg Indian Council which is a council of treaty people in Winnipeg is recognized by the MIB and sits on its board] we are not recognized by Indian Affairs and cannot get any money from them. I think that's discrimination. Just because we live in a city doesn't make us any less treaty."

The real disappointment about Neeginan seems to come through between the lines from all its actors and critics. Here was the chance to do something forceful and positive and dramatic about an equally dramatic situation. It was the opportunity to do something highly imaginative as a demonstration not only to native people and to the city of Winnipeg, but to cities everywhere. And the opportunity was blown. The problem is not simply that Neeginan as it was conceived by the feasibility study was never built; the extravagance of that conception may well have been part of the problem. But all the predictable things happened. Governments gave generous monies for a study and then backed off from pursuing the suggestions that came out of the study. Consultants and planners saw a gravy train in the making and promptly took over the show. The temptation to go with architecture was too much to resist, so concrete and mortar rather than purpose became the focus of the discussion. The native leadership which had initiated the idea held together for awhile and then, as frustration upon frustration set in, slowly deflated and disappeared. So Neeginan, that had started out with such high hopes, quickly became the village that never was. And, sadly, because the idea of Neeginan was carried so far, it can now be trotted out, like the Edsel, as a good excuse never to venture again.

Housing That Works

With the exception of some space for senior citizens and for transients that would have been built into the Community Services Centre, housing for native people was not part of Neeginan, at least as it was conceived by the consultants in their final report. Neeginan very early shied away from the question of housing in favour of concentrating efforts around the Community Services Centre. In doing this, the planners felt they were responding to the cynicism of native people about yet another survey or yet another initiative in the housing field. As the report said, "Another reason for the preference of the delegates for the services centre building over housing is the fact that the native people are fed up with housing surveys and discussions, and are cynical about promises of improved housing conditions. The issue of housing is probably the most exploited of all the issues affecting the native people who are still, for the most part, without decent housing."

So Neeginan, rather than being projected as a complete and self-contained "village", became a service and cultural centre and stayed away from housing at the insistence of native people. This was in spite of the fact that, according to the report, "generally speaking, the Indians and Métis continue to be poorly housed....The evidence which emerged during the study process indicated that there are still large numbers of families and single persons who are housed in sub-standard accommodation, and improvement in this situation is being effected very slowly and only on a limited scale."

There are a couple of ways, however, that native people can get special dispensation in urban housing. One is an Indian Affairs program called the Off-Reserve Housing Program. Needless to say, it is only for treaty Indians, and not for non-status or Métis people. The Off-Reserve Housing Program is governed under the National Housing Act of 1954 and is available to treaty Indians throughout Canada. Essentially, it involves a loan made on the basis of the applicant's income and hence abilities to meet monthly mortgage payments. A grant is also provided to the applicant for furnishings. The Off-Reserve Housing Program is geared to assist stable and upwardly mobile people to purchase a house.

A more extensive program in Winnipeg (with a counterpart in Edmonton) is designed to rent housing to native people. The program in Winnipeg is called Kinew and receives lavish praise at most turns. Kinew started in 1970 as an experiment of the Indian and Métis Friendship Centre in co-operation with Central Mortgage and Housing Corporation. It was incorporated as a non-profit corporation, and, with hundred per cent CMHC financing, initially bought seventeen houses. Kinew now has 150 houses with a market value of over four million dollars. It attempts to salvage old houses employing native tradesmen, trained on the job, to do any required renovations. Kinew then rents the houses at a rent based on the applicant's ability to pay, with a government subsidy making up the difference. Average rents in 1979 were $190 for three- and four-bedroom houses. Welfare recipients make up sixty per cent of Kinew tenants and the houses are spread throughout four areas of Winnipeg. Kinew's board of directors is entirely native.

These are two housing programs. The Off-Reserve Housing Program provides loans, mortgage assistance, and grants for furnishings. But it provides these only to treaty Indians, and only to families that demonstrate stability and motivation. It is a program for the native people who are *not* having trouble adjusting to the city. For them it is good. But they are the ones who need help least.

Programs like Kinew are more broadly based: they are available to all native people; they are rental programs and are more immediate to people in need. But Kinew in Winnipeg has a waiting list of five hundred names.

So while both programs take stabs at the housing needs of native people in the cities, and while both are successful within their own terms of reference, adequate, affordable housing is still a crying need among large numbers of urban native people.

Economics is likely the largest factor in native people's housing problems; native people in inadequate housing suffer because they are too poor to afford to buy or rent better. What is affordable to them is only what is shoddy, draughty, unattractive, and too small.

Stanley McKay, from his own experiences and from his work with the United Church, agrees that the first major problem encountered by a native person in the city is housing. "On the reserve," he says "there is this idea of sharing; there's always room for one more, nobody is left out on the street. Here in the city it is different." McKay relates the story of a family who moved to the city and rented a house. When a relative came to town with his family but had no place to stay, he showed up on the family's doorstep. Naturally they took him in. But the landlord found out and pointed out that he had only rented the house to one family. Both families were thrown into a quandary. Not knowing what to do, they did nothing. The landlord became exasperated and evicted everyone. So then there were two families out on the street looking for a place to stay. McKay says, "This is very difficult for an Indian person who has been brought up in the Indian value system to all of a sudden say to his friends, 'sorry, I can't help you out, you have to find your own place.'"

Two problems are relative to this story. One is overt discrimination. In every city I visited I heard over and over the stories of landlord's refusals to rent to native people. Or the resistance of white neighbourhoods to have a native family move onto the block. This discrimination usually takes its rationale from the discriminator having had a bad experience with a native tenant in the past, or from having heard about someone else who had a bad experience with a native tenant. So the prejudice becomes generalized and no native person stands a chance of living on those premises. Human rights legislation notwithstanding, people *are* discriminated against in housing on the basis of being native.

The other problem is also one that might be termed a discrimination problem though it is an unwitting one. City housing, particularly newer city housing, is not designed or built for a large or an extended family. Twelve people who wanted to live together under one roof would have great difficulty in finding a place to accommodate them in a modern city like Winnipeg, Edmonton, or Regina. Housing is designed and built for groups of four or five people. Public housing in Winnipeg has a maximum of four bedrooms. So if a native family wants to live with children, cousins, and grandparents, the accepted custom on reserves or in rural communities, and still have room for visitors who want to stay for extended periods of time, they would be precluded from doing so simply by the design of the housing that in the city they are more and more restricted to.

There are three housing needs for native people in a city like Winnipeg. Needs that will have to be met both for the comfort and well-being of native people, and for the health of the city if it is to accommodate itself to the fact of the large native population. The cities in general need better quality low-income housing so that everybody can live within their means but still in some degree of comfort and safety. The cities need orientation facilities for new migrants, of the sort first envisioned in the idea for Neeginan, and they need emergency short-term housing for transient people, both families and singles. And the cities need housing that acknowledges the cultural fact that large families and extended families will want to live together.

There are not large orders, but they are critical to meeting needs in an otherwise crisis-filled area.

Reserve Photographs by John Paskievich

Three Women in Regina

I meet the three women sitting around a table upstairs in a house on Dewdney Street. They are middle-aged women. But they are students as well. They are involved in a six-month course financed by a provincial government grant for women on welfare.

What they are engaged in is called the "Community Awareness Project", a large and a hopeful name, and a program of the Regina Native Community Awareness Society. The course is intensive; they spend hours each day in this room talking about themselves, trying to learn about themselves, trying to learn about the community around them, and trying to learn the skills that will allow them in turn to counsel others who are in their position. They are shy women who for a long time are slow to answer and then answer only softly in one word or short sentences. We talk for a long while before they relax. They are women whose life histories read like long sad litanies of poverty and grief; uprooted existences, failed marriages, bouts with drinking, a terrified existence for one with a husband who beat her frequently, lives governed by fear at almost every turn; fear of families, fear of husbands, fear of white people, fear of the world around them, fear of officials, fear of want and poverty, fear of saying the wrong thing.

When they are finished this course, they presume that they will know themselves somewhat better, that they will know their way with some confidence and self-assurance through the jungle of the social service world and that they will be sophisticated enough and aggressive enough to help others who are like they once were. They are optimistic. They believe that they have nowhere to go but up, and they are both happy and relieved that they are at last making the move. We started by talking about the concern the women had for the futures of their children, particularly their worries about the high school drop-out rate among native students.

Edith

I have one daughter in school. She's fourteen. She goes to a pretty good school. She's been going to this school for three years and so far it's the school she likes best. I've had trouble with teachers, though. My daughter was going to a school where she was a minority. Not only were there not many natives, there weren't many Negroes or many Chinese. In my girl's class she was the only native and there was one Chinese boy and the teachers always picked on them, used them for examples. If he had a funny joke to make about an Indian, he always used her for the example. He was always making jokes about her and Danny, Danny was the Chinese boy. He'd come into the classroom sometimes pretending to talk Chinese and all the kids would laugh but it would hurt Danny's feelings. Or the teacher would call Danny a "rice paddy". One time he called Rhonda, my girl, a "wagon burner". She came home and told me. Nobody had ever called her that before. I guess he called her that because being an Indian they used to do that long ago with their bows and arrows. She told me about it. She said that the teacher had just laughed and said, "Don't take such offence." But, she said, "I did." It was like he was trying to turn all these kids who had been her friends against her. Of course a couple caught on and after that they'd call her a "wagon burner" too.

I knew that she always did her homework because she would always bring her books home and show them to me so that I would know how she was getting along with her work. She would always bring her tests home too so we would know how she had done. One time she brought home her tests, it was from the first exams of the year, I guess it was the Christmas exams. All the parents had to sign the tests and then they would take them back to the school. Anyway she brought all her papers home and we looked at them all. Her lowest mark was in social studies, I think. It was about sixty-three. You know, she's not exactly a genius or anything but she had some seventies maybe a couple of eighties. So I knew she had all these marks and we signed the papers and she took them back. A week later she brought home her report card and on her report card she had nothing but Ds and Es. Those are all failing marks. She was mad, she was crying. And she said, "Dad, Mom, you've seen all my tests and this is what the teacher gave me. He gave me all failing marks when my tests were all passing marks. You've seen them."

So I phoned him and made an appointment to go see him. And I went. I've always gone to see the teachers before and they are always quite friendly and ready to discuss your child. He had everything written down on paper prepared for me. And he wasn't very friendly. He just took the papers and he started reading; "Rhonda hasn't done this and Rhonda hasn't done this and this and this and this . . ." I stopped him and I told him, "There must be something good about my child, I've never had these problems before." I told him, "I don't care how bad a student is or how many problems they have, there must be something good about them, at least one good thing. There can't be everything bad."

Then I asked him about her report card. I showed him the report card and asked to see all her tests again because I wanted to compare the marks on the tests against the marks on the report card. Then he told me that Rhonda had never turned her test papers back in to him. But I told him that I had seen them all and had signed them all and that I knew that Rhonda had been with three of her girlfriends and that they had all turned their test papers back in at the same time. I told him that I had already asked these three other children, they were white girls, if Rhonda had turned her papers in because I wanted to make sure that I wasn't coming there with false information. Then he said that he was sorry but if she turned the papers in he must have misplaced them and he would have to look for them. So I told him, "There's something wrong here because a minute ago you were telling me you were so sure that she hadn't turned them in and now you say that you must have misplaced them."

Then I told him about some of things she had told me, how he always used her and Danny the Chinese boy for the class cartoon. And he got mad. He sat up and he said, "I've taught native children before and none of the parents have ever come here and spoken to me like that." He was telling me to stay in my place and not to talk to him like that. But I said to him, "One of the reasons why parents have not spoken up for their children is that when they get them into a good school that their child enjoys, if that native parent comes to the school and raises a stink at the school they know that it will only make it harder on their child, that the teachers will make it hard on their child and maybe their child will drop out." That is what a lot of us are afraid of so we don't speak up.

Virginia

I think that usually it's easier to live in a neighbourhood where there are other native people. My sister lives near to where I live and we help each other out. Also our kids go to the same school. We've been there long enough that I've got to know one of the teachers at the school and she says whenever I think that there are any problems I should come and talk to her.

Rose

Living close to other native people is both good and bad. I have two younger children, one is eleven and one is eight. The rest are all fifteen and up. My sister lives just next door to me. And it's hard. Your own sister, younger than you, and when she asks me for help I don't try to turn professional but I do my best to help her. But she's got teenage kids galore and they move right in to our home. At all hours of the night these girls are in and out and that's hard. It's hard to say no to them, but my older boys all have to get up at seven o'clock to go to work. I want my sister to keep her girls at home but she won't. Last night she came to me again because she didn't have enough money for food. But I told her I couldn't help her in that department because I've already tried. I told her, "It's up to you now, that's your home, I don't care if you just rent it, it's still your home, and it's up to you to shut the door on those girls."

Edith

I first came to Regina when I was a young girl. I was going to school but I came during the summer holidays to work. When I finished grade ten I came back and got a job babysitting. I got the job through Miss Drake, the United Church worker. My aunt was already living here and she gave Miss Drake my name and asked if she could get me a job. I worked for a family where the man was Métis but his wife was white. I quit school then because I thought it was pretty good to be making some money. I stayed with that family for about two and a half years.

Then when I was seventeen I got a job in this restaurant. The boss was Chinese and asked me if I'd like to be a waitress. He said he'd been watching me when I had been coming in to the restaurant and he said he thought I looked like I was honest. He said if I would work hard, he would train me. I was there for three years.

Rose

I was born and raised on a reserve north of here. When I was fourteen I asked my father if I could go to high school but my mother said "no". Instead they married me off, when I was fourteen, to a man I didn't know. I was very disappointed. I didn't know what I wanted to get into but I knew I wanted to better my education. But they married me off to another reserve. I was there for about ten years. Everything went smoothly for the first two years and when I was seventeen, I had my first child. I was still a teenager but I had to learn to be a wife and mother. And I learned to love my husband in spite of the fact that I didn't know him. But then our troubles started.

I left my husband and I wasn't going to go back. My troubles started to get to me and I started to drink. I drank and drank. I used to go in and out of Regina and I went all over the place. I went into other provinces and I even went down to California. There is a lotta things I did to break down the wall I had built around myself. It was 1970 when I decided to settle in Regina. It wasn't too hard because I had been here before, alone. And then one by one my children came home to me and I had them all together. I was living on welfare and I was always crying for this and that until a couple of years ago I decided to quite crying. I started by looking for work. I went to all the agencies trying to get work but I always had too little education.

I didn't want to go back to working as a dishwasher so I decided to take a course in sewing and I signed up, twenty dollars for eight weeks, to learn to sew. I thought that there would be a lot of treaty Indians but when I got there that first evening I found out that I was the only one. The other women were all white and one Chinese girl. I felt bad when I sat down because the woman I sat beside pushed way over but I thought to myself that I have to stay with it because I have to do something to get off welfare. And I have to teach my children this because if I don't I'll be on welfare for ever and they will too.

One of the lessons was to make a T-shirt. I had only three dollars to buy material and I saw all the expensive material these other women were buying but I thought to myself, I'm going to show you what an Indian woman can do. I bought the cheapest, it wasn't even a dollar's worth of material, and the next week I came in and I sat away from the rest, not like the first time. But the instructor points me out, "Can I see your sewing?" I thought they were going to make fun of me. But I had made my T-shirt to the tee. I took it to her. She inspected it and said that it was very good, I had done everything just the way she had taught me. She passed it around and it went through the hands of all of them. And I sort of felt bad because all these real rich women, I don't know if they were rich but they were spending money like crazy on this real fancy material, but some of them had such poor sewing. And I felt bad. But afterwards one of them came to me and asked, "How did you do this? What kind of stitch did you use?" And that made me feel good. Then the teacher used me for an example for the whole class. She said, "Rose is the example, she bought cheap material because she knew she was just going to be practising." That made me feel good and after that things got better for me.

Virginia

I didn't come alone to the city because my sister was here in Regina. She's a nurse, a CNA, a Certified Nursing Assistant. I wanted to be a nurse too and they told me that I'd have to come to Regina to have interviews with the people at Pasqua [a Regina hospital]. It used to be the Grey Nuns before. I had to go to the employment office because you had to have pink cards whenever you were going to take any training or apply for a job, or go for an interview. I went to Saskatoon to take training. This was in '61. And I failed, I failed all my exams. You're only allowed to fail so many exams and I failed all of them so I either had to go back to school or else take another trade.

I thought I'd take hairdressing, but at the same time I didn't want to go back to Saskatoon because I was always so lonesome. I didn't want to be away from home. So I came back to Regina and I stayed with my sister for a while.

Then I met my husband. My sister's husband and my husband were brothers. I didn't want to go back to Saskatoon so I got pregnant and between then and '71 I had several children and I lived with my husband. But it took me a while to realize that he was an alcoholic. I had a miserable life with him but I stuck it out as long as I could. He left me in '71. I started to meet other women, white ladies, who helped me out.

Ever since then I've been alone with the children and I've been on welfare. And all that time I hated the idea of being on welfare. There were times when I tried to do something about it; I took day jobs, or another time I took a homemaker's course and that didn't work out so I took another course for three months but that wasn't for me so I quit that too. Finally, I guess it was mostly through the help of my social worker, that I accepted the fact that I should do something about my life, that I should change it. My sister helped me a lot too.

Rose

I don't go to the Friendship Centre anymore. For my part, the Friendship Centre was supposed to be a place where everyone could go to and feel at home. When I was moving around to all the different provinces, I went to different Friendship Centres and they welcomed me in, as a human and as an Indian. But here in Regina, my home city, a lotta times I'd go into the centre thinking I'd get some advice from one of the counsellors but they were no help. I don't know what got into them, power or money, but they don't care what goes on as long as they are taking their money. And they were supposed to be doing good for the people.

A lot of people are bitter about the organizations. For my part, every time I went in there it was as if I wasn't wanted; I had to stand against the wall so that I wouldn't get kicked from behind. There's a feeling in there that makes you feel that you're not wanted without your being told.

I talk both Cree and Saulteaux because my father was Cree and my mother was Saulteaux. My children don't speak any Indian language. They have all been to boarding school. I went to boarding school too and when I went I couldn't speak a word of English though I could speak a little French which I had learned from my grandmother. But my only communication with the other girls was in Cree and Saulteaux which was very wrong in the boarding school. It was run by priests and nuns. So I had to learn myself English.

Then when they started sending the kids to white schools, I thought "What's the use of teaching my kids Indian languages?" though I myself was still using Cree with some of the elderly people. If my children want to learn Indian languages, they'll have to learn it themselves. If they learn it, it's up to them, it's not up to me.

Edith

I'm Assiniboine and I was brought up by my grandparents so I learned how to talk the language from them. But my grandparents are dead now so there is nobody to talk it to anymore. I'm in the city, my husband is white, so we talk English and my daughter talks English. I've taught my daughter a few words in Assiniboine, like "rabbit" and "dog" and "woman" and "man". My girl says that she would like to learn more. But then teenagers are usually busy doing other things.

I still make bannock, though, and my husband likes it and my girl likes it and all her friends like it even though they're white. They like it better than bread. If there is bread and there is bannock they will always eat the bannock. They really like it, the white kids. I talk a lot to my friends and even my cousin who just moved off the reserve and into the city here, her children started to associate with white children here and they would bring them home and everything and she was telling me about when they couldn't afford bread and had to have bannock. And she said, "What do you do when the white kids come to your house, like your kids bring them home and they all want something to eat, and all I have is bannock and I'm always so shy?..." And I told her as far as I'm concerned, eat what we eat, and if they don't like it they can go home and eat. Kids in this day and age more or less accept people for what they are. They don't care how we eat. A long time ago a lot of white children made fun of the Indian people but I notice that that's going away. Kids don't say things like that anymore. When we had cultural days at the university you should have seen the white people there, the kids. We had rabbit stew and bannock and pemmican and they just lined up there like anything. Everybody wanted the Indian food.

Schools

What Happens in the City Happens Here First

Unless a child learns about the forces which shaped him; the history of his people, their values and customs, their language, he will never really know himself or his potential as a human being. Indian culture and values have a unique place in the history of mankind. The Indian child who learns about his heritage will be proud of it. The lessons he learns in school, his whole school experience, should reinforce and contribute to the image he has of himself as an Indian.

National Indian Brotherhood paper on Indian control of Indian education, 1972

Teachers from River Heights roll up at the inner city school in their Mercedes, values and all, and try to teach kids that this is the way it should be without learning anything about the culture the children are from.

an unhappy former teacher (native) in Winnipeg

Of eighty-three schools in Winnipeg's sprawling School Division Number One, a division that covers all of the old city and parts of some of the northern suburbs, thirty-six have significant native enrolments. A conservative estimate places six thousand children who identify themselves as native in this school division, twenty per cent of the total school enrolment. A handful of schools in the core of the city have native enrolments that exceed fifty per cent and are as high as eighty per cent.

The case in Regina is similar. A 1976 study by the Department of Indian Affairs put the school-age population, between five and nineteen years of age, of people of Indian ancestry in Regina at 9,782 or twenty-three per cent of the city's school-age population. As in Winnipeg there are numerous schools in Regina with significant native enrolments and several schools, particularly in the part of the city known as the north central area, where native enrolment is over fifty per cent.

In both cities the school systems reacted late to the novelty of these visibly different children that were making up a rapidly increasing proportion of their school populations. Despite the sincerity of individual teachers, schools themselves are quite impersonal systems that demand a predictable raw product at one end in order to produce an equally predictable finished commodity at the other end. Large urban public schools have infinitely refined ways of moving children through their system. Children move through in groups that are determined on the basis of their age combined with a streaming that is done on the basis of brightness or aptitude. But the object of the schooling is to move the child from point A to point B (and all faculty of education graduates are trained to achieve this) with the necessary assumption being that all children will enter the system at point A.

When the Indian children started pouring into this system, they screwed up the works. The Indians were different. They weren't predictably *at* point A. Education specialists didn't know for certain where many of them fitted in at all. Some couldn't speak English or spoke it with difficulty. Some had never been to a city until the day they arrived at the school's front door. Many were totally disoriented in their urban environment. Many, particularly in the inner city, were poor, living almost hand-to-mouth. Many had parents who were even more wide-eyed and less city-wise than they were. Yet these children were arriving at the schools in large numbers. The schools didn't know what to do. For a while they tried to act as if nothing was amiss, then, predictably, they started blaming the kids.

Educators trotted out the theories about the importance of pre-school life to later school success — the parents must talk in certain ways, the child must have had certain experiences, the child must have developed a questioning mind, etc. One school principal, in pained sincerity and at great length, talked about the factors external to the school that impeded learning in the children in his over-sixty-per-cent native school. The kids were deprived. If they were poor, they were economically deprived, they couldn't have had creative playthings as tiny tots to spur enquiring minds. Or they did not have a diet that could keep bodies awake and minds alert. If they were native they were culturally deprived. They didn't understand the city, at least the one the school system understood. Or they couldn't put words to concepts. Or they didn't have ingrained competitive or aggressive values. Frequently they were seen as deprived on both counts. The education system is predicated on the uniformity and the predictability of the raw product. The native children weren't right, they weren't what the system needed.

The system tried to tinker with the kids, tried to make them right. The psychologists were called in. They confirmed what the system had believed; the children were not quite right. Too frequently the children were labelled slow or retarded and were streamed accordingly. Some schools made brave attempts at breakfast programs or pre-school orientations. Mostly they threw up their hands. The children failed. They still do. And they dropped out. In both Regina and Winnipeg there is a massive drop-out of native children at the junior-high level.

They get fed up. By this time they have what educators call an "accumulated skills deficit" that is almost impossible to overcome and rests with them as a severe source of frustration. More directly, as one school principal put it, "They're not stupid. By this time they know that they are the under-class and that they're not going anywhere." Based on past experience the Manitoba Indian Brotherhood projected that in 1980 only ten per cent of Indian children who started school in 1967–68 would graduate from grade twelve. The graduating percentage among all Manitobans is ninety per cent. The Indian kids have failed.

So has the school system.

Two Cities, Two Schools
The painful first attempts

Through the fence I watch the little girl. She stands in the schoolyard — tense, immobile, feet wide apart on the dusty hard-packed ground where most of the dried grass has been worn away. One running shoe lace is untied, the strings trailing haphazardly along the side of her foot. She holds the brown soccer ball close to her stomach with the fingers of both hands spread wide for a better grip. She does not move, partly in tension, partly because the rules of the game as explained by the tall young woman standing, shivering slightly, and watching from the sidelines are that you can't run until you've thrown the ball. But her face glows with excitement. Her mouth is fixed in a wide smile that exposes her incisors newly grown-in and the hole where another adult cuspid is still to come. Her black eyes shine, only partly aware of the details around her, seeing mostly a blur of bodies running in every direction awaiting the throw of the ball, the ball that will nail one of them who will then be "it". The blonde-haired girl, the little boy with freckles and cowboy boots, the little kid whose skin is dark as chocolate, the little Chinese girl. The girl still holds the ball and the wind blows her silky black hair across her face. Her arms go up. And she throws it. Suddenly the whole playground around her bursts into a flurry and she too is in the action, running, into the dust and the wind and the screams of the other children.

This is Regina. This is Albert Elementary School. It is difficult to conceive that this little girl, observed in the innocence of her play, could be aware of the clash of rancour and struggle and disappointment, and finally of grudging accommodation, that she and her brothers and sisters and playmates have recently been the subject of in her school. Albert School, a yellow fortress of bricks looming behind the playground, is one of the older schools in Regina. It was built in 1907 and now sits fenced off from the rows of tall lean frame houses squashed together and the little corner groceries run by people whose names — Boyko, or Sam Lee — are printed under 7-Up signs. It is a neighbourhood of bumpy sidewalks, and adult elm trees whose leaves fall and blow into corners behind bicycle racks. Down the street and across a much more busy street, is the shadow of the city's football stadium.

Albert School has 320 children. Perhaps 140 of these are native children. Rob Inglis, the school's vice-principal, says that four years ago there were hardly any native children at Albert School. In January of 1979 Albert School took a novel step in Regina, it placed three native women as classroom assistants in primary classes. The classroom assistants were para-professionals, not professional teachers. The requirements were that they be of native ancestry, that they live in the community that was close to the school, and that they have a knowledge of native cultural background. The Regina Board of Education called it a pilot project and sat back to watch how it worked.

The three young women work in primary classrooms helping the white teachers. One taught a grade three class to make bannock. Another brought in an Indian elder to tell stories to the children. Sometimes, if the regular teacher is busy with the rest of the class, they will spend time with a child who is having difficulties with reading. They all say, "If we teach anything, it has to be within the cultural sphere because otherwise we're not qualified." Vice-principal Inglis is very happy. He's sure the program is there to stay and that it will expand into other schools.

Not so happy are Linda Hudson and Teresa Stevenson.

I sit in a house two blocks from Albert School and drink tea with Linda Hudson and Teresa Stevenson. Linda Hudson used to teach at Albert School. She is white. Teresa Stevenson is Saulteaux. She was born on a reserve near Broadview, Saskatchewan, but also lived for twenty years with her husband, Bob, in a small town in Montana. Now, in her mid-fifties, she has lived in Regina since 1970. Early in 1978 Teresa Stevenson and Linda Hudson began to agitate for schools that would be more responsive to the native children in their midst and that would also be more inclined to talk to — and to listen to — neighbourhood parents, what they called "the community". Up to that point the Regina school system had responded haphazardly to the growing numbers of native children. They had identified "problems" and had tried to react to them. For example, they had identified attendance (or lack of it) as a problem and had hired community workers who were in fact truant officers to deal with it. For Hudson and Stevenson this was neither the right approach, nor did it go far enough. The problem as Teresa Stevenson saw it, was fundamental. There was little or nothing in the school experience that the children could see as valuable or relevant. And there was little or no attempt to include parents in the discussions about what school for their children should be. So the kids got bored with it all and dropped out. And the parents had no reason for encouraging them to stay. To underline her point Stevenson remarked that her three sons, who had been schooled when the family lived in Montana, had all graduated from high school as a matter of course. In Regina, by contrast, an Indian high school graduate was rare indeed.

In 1978 Stevenson and Hudson, then still a teacher at Albert School, formed an education committee as a subcommittee of a local community society, the North Central Community Society. Together with a United Church worker and with the support of a native society in the community, the Riel Creesaulteaux Society, they began to enlist support from parents and to lobby with the school authorities. They first asked for two things; that the school principals and teachers become better acquainted with the communities in which they taught, less hit and run — in at nine in the morning and back to the suburbs at four; and they wanted native teachers, particularly in schools with high enrolments of native children. The school board answered that if they could hire native teachers, they would. But it was difficult to find any who were qualified. The committee then proposed native teaching assistants who would be hired by the board to work in schools with large native enrolments, and who, by working, would gain in training and experience. The school board countered by asking the committee to propose a pilot project for *one* school and let that prove itself before it was expanded. The committee picked its local school, Albert School.

It was from there that things started to break

down. The committee expanded to include a professor and a community college teacher and it attempted to meet at Albert School with school staff in attendance. The school principal and then the staff felt threatened. The gap between Linda Hudson and the principal and staff at Albert School widened. The committee heard themselves called disparaging names, "radicals" and "street people". Teachers at Albert School who had expressed interest began to withdraw. But the committee continued its work and in the autumn of 1978 it presented a proposal to the board of education to provide native trainees to primary classes at Albert School. The selected candidates would receive training on the job, would liase with parents and the community, would be in charge of all Indian content for the class, would have an outside co-ordinator, and would be supported by an advisory committee that would include a school board administrator, resource people, and people from the community. The proposal was submitted to the board of education *without* the support of Albert School's principal.

Now the school board balked. The community committee wanted the program to be controlled by the community; they didn't want it to be solely under the jurisdiction of a principal. The school board and its administrators saw the program as getting beyond their control. A power struggle ensued with a series of heated meetings during one of which the chairman of the school board is reported to have said that the Indians should pull themselves up by their bootstraps like the Ukrainians did. The politics got so involved that a nervous Riel Creesaulteaux Society withdrew support from the proposal.

In the end, the school board won. In January 1979 they hired three aides for Albert School. But they called them classroom assistants. They were to be controlled by the school system and co-ordinated by a consultant to the board of education. In order to implement the program, both the principal at Albert School and Linda Hudson were transferred from Albert School in June of 1978.

Linda Hudson and Teresa Stevenson complain about their loss. They are discouraged and disappointed. They complain that those hired were young women who became, by implication, the most junior staff at the school. They say that they needed to hire older, stronger, more aggressive aides. They say that they needed the outside co-ordinator to make sure that "Indian things really happened" at the school. They are not sure that the present program will make much of a difference.

"Winnipeg waited too long. The tidal wave is right behind our backs; we're running and looking over our shoulder at it." George Heshka is the principal of Dufferin School, an older red brick school just north and just west of downtown Winnipeg with its back up against the CPR tracks. The native enrolment at Dufferin School is around eighty per cent. Heshka: "This school division didn't realize until three years ago that everything was changing under their feet. To give them credit, they responded quickly. But it took them a long time to realize it. In ten years Winnipeg Number One will be an inner-city school division entirely. The boys at head office just caught on to that."

We are walking down a corridor in Dufferin School past a long, brilliantly coloured mural of water and tipis and elaborately drawn mythical fish characters. Heshka has a reputation as an innovative and outspoken man. He is also a frustrated and angry man. Community worker Gerry Recksiedler, who works out of the school, is walking with us. This afternoon he will travel to city hall to continue a push that Dufferin School is in no small way responsible for, to get the city to take an initiative in inner-city non-profit housing.

Heshka elaborately draws the inter-connections. The school cannot function in a vacuum. "The kids who come here have the problems of poverty compounded by problems of cultural differences," he says. If a child's basic nutrition and housing needs are not met, a school doesn't make much sense for him. Operating a school against those odds is a frustrating endeavour. At Dufferin some things have worked, some things haven't worked. Many things are still being tried.

Four years ago the school was the site of an attempt at an all-native school, a school within a school. There were four classes at the primary level; all native students, all native teachers. The teachers were to create the curriculum. The school was called *Anishinibanse*. It failed in a little over a year. Heshka came to Dufferin just as the experiment was ending. He believes it failed because nobody wanted it to work badly enough. It was staffed with first-year teachers fresh out of college, who were given little support.

Heshka claims some success with different teaching methods such as a cell approach to reading. The approach was developed in ghetto schools in large American cities and has had remarkable success with older children. At Dufferin the school has taken the initiative to develop parent councils. One of Gerry Recksiedler's tasks is to organize the parent councils that meet once a month to discuss anything from traffic lights to glue-sniffing problems. At Dufferin there is a profound sense that the school cannot function all by itself, oblivious to the life in the community around it.

Bob Davies is a consultant to inner-city schools in Winnipeg's School Division Number One. For the past three years he has been making a concerted effort to get the schools to work with native children. He lists what has happened. In 1975 a native aide program was started at Machray School in the city's north end. By 1979 fourteen such aides were employed by the school division. The job of an aide is to visit homes, interpret school programs to parents, work with children who have special problems, and ensure attendance. For a while twenty additional aides were employed on a Canada Works grant provided through the Indian and Métis Friendship Centre. (They were let go when the grant period ended in 1979.) In 1978 a Native Advisory Committee to the board of education was established with representatives from a variety of native organizations. In 1979 the school division hired a native educational consulting teacher to aid schools and collect teaching resources. In 1979 at the impetus of a committee of the United Church, a series of workshops on native culture and attitudes were instituted for principals and teachers from thirty-six schools with large native enrolments. Six half-day workshops were held, followed by three days of in-service training around native issues.

And yet in Winnipeg, as in Regina, there remains every indication that the school system continues to fail native children. The drop-out rate at the junior-high level remains extraordinarily high. The hopeful little children who trot bright-eyed into kindergarten have grown up quickly; they are jaded and bored and have abandoned hope. In June of 1979 Sherry Farrell, a native consulting teacher with the Winnipeg School Division Number One, surveyed a number of older native students about their school-related concerns. She prefaced her report of the survey with the comments of a couple of students, one of whom had pointed out to her the number of educational and social service professionals who get their pay cheques from his difficulties, and another who complained about the wealth of native-awareness workshops available to adults while the native students themselves "couldn't even find a meaningful book in their library".

The answers to the questions were interesting and revealing, though the survey covered a small sample. Of twenty-six students interviewed less than half said that English was the language spoken at home; sixteen had attended more than four schools; seventeen complained of having experienced prejudice or discrimination at the hands of other students; sixteen admitted that they did not enjoy school; twenty-one felt it was very important to learn about their native culture and history; twenty-three said that they would sign up if native language classes were offered at their school; and when asked to select the sort of school they would like to attend, almost half, twelve students, said that they would prefer to go to a school that was for Indian and Métis students only and which had an emphasis on native culture, job skills, and native languages.

Ms. Farrell pointed out that although native students were infrequently asked their opinions about their schooling, their feelings are often eloquently expressed in classrooms everywhere, "with actions that vary from disruptive to withdrawn to non-attendance they voice their dissatisfaction with their school experiences."

The dilemma of the urban schools is a significant one. The experience at Albert School in Regina was the result of grass-roots organizing by the parents to move the school board to introduce a native component into the program of an integrated school. In Winnipeg there was a late recognition of the native fact in inner-city schools, a flurry of in-service cultural training for teachers, the flirtation with a special school, and the acknowledgement that, again particularly in inner-city schools, poverty as well as culture is an influential factor.

But through it all nobody has yet answered a fundamental question about native children in urban public school systems. A young native teacher described the nursery school materials that were available to her in her predominantly native classroom; the puppets were all of white people, the language charts involved white people doing urban and suburban things, household utensils were strange to a child newly arrived from a reserve, and life in general was depicted as the North American stereotype; Anglo-Saxon families of two and three children (not twelve as was the experience of a number of children in her class). The question remains — should the schools adjust to native children by developing a curriculum and methods of teaching that better acknowledge native heritage, history, culture, art, and music; a curriculum that re-evaluates the place of native people in the history of the continent? Or should the priority be, as one teacher put it, to teach the skills to cope with an urban life?

The public schools move ponderously in any direction. In a few cases, Calgary and Toronto for example, all-native schools have started by themselves. Though the Toronto school, called Wandering Spirit Survival School, is now accepted as an alternative school by the Toronto Board of Education, the school program, replete with Sacred Circle of Life ceremonies and sweetgrass smoke rituals, makes it function much more in the way of a religious parochial school. The public schools tend to shy away from anything that seems segregationist, with the brief exception of Anishinibanse in Winnipeg. Educators who favour native content within an integrated school argue that not only should native children see things of their heritage taken seriously and explored, white children should likewise be placed in the position to challenge their stereotypes. Even the significance of having native teachers for classrooms with native children is debated. In Winnipeg George Heshka says; "If you are talking straight learning expertise, it makes no difference." Yet he is quick to add, "If you are talking sociological impact or how a community sees a school, it is important, so they don't see just white faces and see the school as just another one of those establishment, colonizing institutions."

What happens in the schools is important; not only for their own sake, but in as much as the schools are a sort of bellwether for many other things in the city. Given the preponderance of young among the urban native population it is almost necessary to say "as go the schools, so goes the city". If the first generation of urban native young people has to live through a school experience that is frustrating, boring, irrelevant, intimidating, and which drives too many of them ultimately to become trouble makers, or to leave, then the future, not only for Indian people in the city but for the cities themselves, is not bright.

The schools are in a difficult position. The pressures on them are enormous. And yet they are in an enviable position because their mandate is so clear cut. Their task is to take essentially bright and eager children and to encourage both their brightness and their eagerness, as well as their security about who they are, and who their forefathers were, and who they might become. If they can do all that, there is indeed reason for hope. If they become instead simply the first of many institutions that persuade the child that there is no room for him, that he is in fact wasting his time, that there are already two strikes against him and that it is just a matter of time before he takes the third; then woe betide us all.

Stanley McKay Sr., Winnipeg

Stanley McKay came to Winnipeg when few other Indian people had ventured there, in 1959. He was forty-eight years old. Before that, he had been a fisherman and had worked in a general store at Fisher River, the Cree community where he had been born, one hundred and fifty kilometers north of Winnipeg.

"My heritage," he says, "is Indian. But it is not my culture." He describes how he never saw an Indian costume; beads and feathers and buck-skins, nor saw a so-called traditional Indian dance until after he moved to Winnipeg, when he was almost fifty years old. He offers that as an honest attempt to sort out the often confused maze of race, heritage, and culture, words that are too often ill-defined and incorrectly used. Obviously at Fisher River the men didn't wear buckskins and feathers when they got into their boats to head out into the often choppy waters of Lake Winnipeg to fish for a living. At least in Stanley McKay's time they didn't. And when the people at Fisher River had a dance it was, as often as not, and as in any other rural Manitoba community, a square dance or some awkward two-step to the accompaniment of a fiddle.

Now Stanley McKay lives in one of Winnipeg's northeastern suburbs on a street of new split-level and bungalow homes; a street with the enticingly pristine name of Greenvalley Bay though there is no valley and the neighbourhood is so new that little has had a chance as yet to grow green.

Mr. McKay is now sixty-seven but is a robust, active, and engaging man who could be taken easily for a dozen years younger. He is retired from a job he held for over fifteen years, running a reception lodge owned by the United Church that accommodated native people who would come into Winnipeg for medical attention. But he does not seem to sit well with idleness. He eagerly maintains an interest in current issues. He was, until recently, head of the Winnipeg Indian Council, the closest Winnipeg has ever come to having a tribal organization. And he eagerly maintains an interest in two young sons. Five children from his first marriage are long grown and scattered from Saskatchewan to Ottawa. The two boys, seven and nine, who are active in his kitchen this day are from his second marriage. He took them and his wife (who is white) to his old reserve at Fisher River this summer so that they could camp out and so that he could teach them to fish and shoot a rifle.

I'm still a member of the Fisher River band. I still get my five dollars a year. I guess I still could go back to the reservation if I wanted to. But I moved to the city in 1959. On the reserve my main livelihood was commercial fishing. Part of the year I would work in the local store as well, at busy times, when it was time to take stock and so on. And for our last seven years on the reserve I worked at the store on a permanent basis. The biggest reason why I moved to the city was that all our children were leaving home. They had to at that time in order to further their education. They were all leaving home and going to residential schools. The first two started off in Brandon. But I wanted to be in a place where I could be in close contact so that I could encourage them.

When we were on the reserve it was very difficult, we'd only see them for the summer holidays and at Christmas. But if you stayed on the reserve there wasn't much encouragement to continue with education. Our opportunities were, in the white man's words, limited.

I was adopted when I was quite young by my uncle and aunt. My uncle passed away when I was sixteen so I had to quit school and go to work. But I'd already reached grade eight and couldn't go any further. That's when I started fishing. So I moved to the city to make it easier for my children.

Before I left the reserve and decided to come to the city, Indian Affairs had a man working in the office here as a placement officer. He was supposed to find employment for any Indian people who wanted to go to the city. He was out on the reserve one time and I met with him and he told me that I wouldn't have any problem finding a job in Winnipeg. So that gave me some encouragement. So we moved.

For the first while I waited, I wasn't too interested in going out on my own to find a job, I was kind of depending on this guy to help me out. He had told me he could get me an office job where I wouldn't have to work long hours, after five o'clock. So I waited because I figured he could get me a better job than I could ever get on my own. In the meantime my wife got a job with the Friendship Centre which was just starting up at that time. So this helped out. Of course we had a little money that we had brought with us.

One of the guys from the Friendship Centre took me around to different places to apply for a job on the basis of my experience working at the store. But I didn't have any recommendations and my education wasn't that good so most places said that they didn't have anything available, or that they would call me as soon as there was. Well they still haven't called me so I guess there still isn't anything available. But finally after about a month I called this guy at Indian Affairs and asked him what was happening. Oh, he said, I'll pick you up and take you to the employment office. Well I could have done that myself.

Finally a job came up at Scott-Bathgate [a

candy factory]. There I did just about everything from stock boy, filling shelves, to filling orders. Then I became a packer, filling orders for country stores. My last job there was, I don't know what you'd call it; I was sitting in an office responsible for shipments to branch offices. I didn't like that, that wasn't for me, wearing a tie and a suit. I'd been there for two and a half years. Then I was offered the job by the United Church when the reception lodge opened up. For seven years I was the manager there. Then I became the worker for the United Church with Indian people.

In 1959 when we came in there were some Indian people in Winnipeg, but I guess you could say that there were no special services for them. My thinking has changed since then, but when I first came in I figured that the best way for native people to make it was to get involved with the existing services. I don't believe that anymore. I think there has to be a stepping stone between the reserve and the regular urban society.

When we came to Winnipeg, our son-in-law who was in the air force was living here. They had a suite on Toronto Street. He was being transferred to Churchill so I sublet his place. There were a lot of questions about that from the landlords. I wasn't employed yet, so I guess they were concerned about getting their rent. But we ended up staying there for about two years. Being from the country, we had a few problems. We were living on the third floor but we were used to having a lot of kids around. My wife worked at the Friendship Centre and she would bring kids home with her. And the people downstairs used to complain that we were making too much noise. So I was careful, the next time we moved I made sure we got a basement suite!

At that time the thing that helped me a lot was the Friendship Centre. I think now that the Friend-ship Centre has lost something in becoming too big. I think they'd have done a lot more for the little guy if they had expanded by putting out more drop-in centres or something like that. One of the things that was very important for me was that we were given some responsibility at the Friendship Centre. There was at that time only a staff of two and the programs were all the responsibility of a committee of native people.

The board of directors at that time were all non-Indians. But as volunteers we were responsible for our own programs and this was good. When they expanded the Friendship Centre, when we built it larger out the back, we did the work, a bunch of us would go in after work every night and put in a few hours and we did all the carpenter work. It was the kind of thing where if anybody needed assistance instead of just giving a hand-out, they'd get them to paint a wall or something first. I thought that was good. But then there was more and more money coming into the Friendship Centre in the form of grants and they were hiring more and more staff. They hired a program director which took our volunteer responsibility away from us so we became obsolete. After that we were only responsible for the rules, you know if there was a dance or something going on there, we were the bad guys. But the involvement that centre provided was important. For me, that was the thing that helped me.

Fisher River is still an important place for me. My son, Stanley Jr., is now the United Church minister there. I have a lotta friends there; I still keep in touch. They still seem glad to see me. In fact this summer for the first time we went out there for our holidays. My wife is white but by one of the peculiarities of our laws she too is treaty. We adopted our two boys and they are now seven and nine. One of the things we'd never done was go out camping in isolation. So this summer we bought a boat and motor and went out to Fisher Bay on Lake Winnipeg and went out a few miles and camped. This was quite an experience for them.

One guy at Fisher River gave me the whole works, a net all set up and a box and a couple of anchors and some ropes so we were all set. Those people are still great, still ready to help. I didn't expect to catch much, it was calm and hot, but I said that we'd set it just to see how it's done. The first day we had a half a dozen pickerel and some bass and a fair sized jack. Our problem was that we didn't have any refrigeration. So I said, this is how we used to do it in the old days; and I dug a hole in the ground and we put them in there. The next morning we went out and the net was just loaded.

The boys have always lived in the city, though they were born treaty. Right from the start we tried to make them realize and accept that they were Indian. When I came to the city I was always thinking about equality. But I've changed my thinking because it seems we're all struggling for the top. I guess some are more equal than others! So I always thought that we shouldn't emphasize that we were different. But now I say that we have to realize right from the start that we are different and that we have to accept that there is nothing wrong in being different. In living in this environment you have to know your background and your heritage, but you can't apply all of it here.

In this environment it's still very difficult to be Indian. Our educational material for example is still very biased, it's still discriminating. Our boys don't come home crying and saying "people called me this" or "people discriminated against me," we teach them not to do that. They have to cope on their own. But sometimes I have to ask myself "How long am I going to tell my boys that anybody who discriminates or says these things, doesn't know? How long do I have to make these excuses before my boys grow up either hating themselves because they're Indian or hating the other guy because he discriminates?" When they were small we had a hard time convincing them that they were different because they didn't want to be different; they saw the TV programs and all. But now they accept the fact that they are Indians.

For over a hundred years we have been working with the native people. Whenever anything went wrong, it was the native people's fault. We never looked at the system. For over a hundred years we tried to make the native person into a white man. If you were steadily employed or if you were well-educated, then you had made it. It troubles me to see how a young child in this culture, right from the time they start kindergarten they are burdened with this responsibility that they have to meet a certain goal. You either make it or you don't. You see, in the native culture you don't have that pressure as a child. If you're going to become a hunter, you become a hunter, you never fail. The only difference is that some are better hunters than others. Here you either make the grade or you don't. This comes every day of your life from the time you start school.

When I came to the city I found it very difficult to adjust myself to this way of life. But I realized that if I wanted to live in the society, then I had to adapt. I just can't survive if I try to live my way. The value system used to bother me. It used to bother me to have a freezer that had stuff in it that I didn't need for a few days. That's something we didn't do on the reserve. We didn't, in the olden days, see one guy with plenty to eat and his neighbour with nothing.

I guess that one of the problems now is that

nobody is really talking to the northern people and painting an adequate picture of what life is like in the city. There's not that much preparation in the northern communities for people that come in to the city. Nobody wants to go home and talk about the problems that they have experienced in the city; they just go back and paint a good picture, you know, you tell them that you draw a certain amount of money a month, a good salary, but you never tell them that a lot of that goes for rent and transportation and every other thing. So when it looks so bright, a lot of people want to come out. If you are able to get a good paying job, it is a good place to live, you can have all the conveniences. But if you are unemployed, it's not such a good place to live.

When I was out on the reserve I lived in a certain way and I was in the majority. I never thought of myself as being any different than anybody else. I met non-Indian people on the reserve and I got along very well with them and I made trips into Winnipeg and I felt that I knew my way around. But when I finally moved in, for the first time I knew that I was different, I was Indian. My ways were different and I realized that if I wanted to live in this society, I had to learn to survive, I had to change my ways.

There are some racist attitudes, but they are very subtle. It's very difficult to attack the enemy that you can't see. There have been cases that have been brought up to the Human Rights Commission and so on but it's difficult to get to the point where you can prosecute a person for discrimination. They've tried a number of times. And yet it's there. I guess the biggest problem Indian people face in the city is this stereotyped image that the majority of non-Indian people have of native people, you know, that all native people are drunkards because they see a number of them on Main Street. And when they talk about Indian people doing something it's as if they mean all native people, not just a group. This makes it very difficult for the man that's new in the city who's struggling to make his own way. All we're begging for is to accept me as an individual, accept me for what I am.

Talking about values, I'm not trying to say that one is right and the other is wrong. Just that they are different. In the dominant society the important thing is independence. When you get your paycheque you're supposed to put away some of that money for what we like to call a "rainy day". We never like to be a burden to the rest of society by living on welfare or having to go to somebody for help when we're sick or when we're old. So we try to take care of that by putting something aside. And then we look up to the guy with a lot of property and with a lot of money. In the old Indian custom we also prepared for that rainy day, not by accumulating wealth, but by sharing. The best hunter was the big man in the community. When he's sick, everybody tries to help him. This is the way he tries to prepare for the rainy day or when he's sick or old. And everybody looks up to him; not to the guy who hoards for himself, he's an outcast. This is one of the things that's very difficult for me to give up. Yet if I want to survive in this society, I have to.

Employment

There are no solutions to Indian poverty in Canadian cities — that is the problem.
Edgar J. Dosman in
Indians — The Urban Dilemma

People can talk around it and say that they're not qualified and all; but underneath, they just don't fucking want Indians.
Native employment counsellor, Regina

Where Are All the Bus Drivers?

Winnipeg may have sixty thousand Indian people. Or more. Regina has twenty or thirty thousand and Edmonton perhaps forty thousand. I make my way around the cities and I keep my eyes open for Indian faces. I want to know where, in the course of a day, we meet. Where, in the nine-to-five rush of a city's day do the city and these masses of native people meet? At what points do native people encounter the city? In what ways do their activities and the on-rushing life of the city join?

Native people have flooded into Regina. Yet if one in four or one in five Reginans is Indian, you could be fooled if you expected every fourth or fifth city bus driver or bank teller or grocery store clerk to be a native person. They are not. You would look hard to find one who is a school teacher or a nurse or a secretary. An official in one of the native bureaucracies related how he had once been asked by someone from the civil service why it was so difficult for a native person to get a job in Regina. The Indian turned the question around and asked the civil servant how many people he thought worked for the federal, provincial, and municipal civil services in Regina. He said that he thought about five thousand. The Indian asked how many of that five thousand were native people. He didn't know. If they followed the twenty per cent figure, there would be a thousand native people employed in the civil service in Regina.

"He said, no we don't have that." I said, "Well, I'll make it easy for you. Do you have a hundred?" He said, "Well, I don't think so." So I said, "How about ten?" He said, "I'm sure we have that."

The reports of a hundred statisticians confirm that there is a shockingly high rate of unemployment for native people both nationally and in the cities. The Department of Indian Affairs estimates that the unemployment rate among people of Indian ancestry in the province of Saskatchewan in 1976 was 36.8 per cent. A study completed in 1979 by Trent University professor Donald McCaskill that compared the urbanization of Canadian Indians in Winnipeg, Toronto, Edmonton, and Vancouver concluded: "the majority of Indians in large Canadian cities exhibit low levels of economic adjustment. High unemployment rates, low incomes, and heavy reliance on social assistance imply that a stable economic existence is beyond the reach of most urban migrants." A 1979 study by the Winnipeg school division decided that unemployment rates in the Winnipeg inner city, where most native people live, were at least fifty-five per cent. A University of Winnipeg Urban Institute study (Winnipeg's Core Area — 1975) points out that in 1971 the average male wage in that same inner city was 30.2 per cent lower than the Winnipeg city-wide average. The report also stated that the disparity

was growing as the 1971 figure was up 6 per cent from a decade earlier when the gap was only 24.4 per cent. In Regina a survey undertaken in 1979 by a city church, Wesley United Church, discovered that only 1.8 per cent of the work force in fifty-four city firms and institutions was native. Among them, the fifty-four firms and institutions employed 55,436 people. In the report by Ken Svenson; *Indian and Métis Issues in Saskatchewan to 2001* (Department of Indian Affairs, 1978) the author points out that in order to reduce the unemployment rate among people of Indian ancestry in Saskatchewan from an estimated 36.8 per cent in 1976 to 12.5 per cent in 2001, 35 per cent of the net increase in jobs between 1976 and 1986 must go to people of Indian ancestry as must 62 per cent of the net increase between 1986 and 2001.

I look in Regina for Indian people at work. With few exceptions I find them in a handful of places. They work for native organizations either in social service or administrative posts directed at service to their own people. They form the staff at the Regina Friendship Centre or at the offices of the Federation of Saskatchewan Indians or the Association of Métis and Non-Status Indians of Saskatchewan. They are the twenty-four-hour-a-day Indians whose race and roles interact so closely that they are almost one and the same thing. Sometimes this is satisfying; or it can be an isolating, segregated life.

There are Indian women who are stenographers in the offices of the Department of Indian Affairs. And there are Indian persons working in the plethora of little, often short-term "projects" concerned with everything from counselling women to entertaining children to rescuing men from jail. These dozens of short-term projects provide tenuous jobs with low pay and scant security. Funding is a magic word. People who work for the projects are always worried about the state of their funding.

From time to time the projects achieve some things with the constituencies they are directed at; more often they have neither the time nor the resources they need and are treated with cynicism from within and without. By the time a staff is hired and an office organized there is only a month left to jockey for an extension of "funding". What the projects do best is provide a fluid source of employment for the Indian person who is motivated to keep at it and sophisticated enough to land a job. Often these jobs are seen primarily as training and may in fact be financed with that explicitly spelled out; they are make-work programs that are of more benefit to whoever is lucky enough to land the job than to anyone else. Buying time is a term that is used frequently when such programs are initiated. Buying time or maybe buying off.

Otherwise there are few places one finds more than the occasional Indian person at work. There are Indian men and boys in the lines waiting for casual work and day labour in the early hours of the dawn, ready to get in a van and ride to a construction yard to unload eighty-pound sacks of cement all day for minimum wage. And there are Indian men hanging around the beer parlours in the last block of Hamilton Street or along South Railway Street. In summer there are men on the benches or lying in the grass in Victoria Park panhandling half-heartedly for a bottle of wine or just sitting talking among themselves. There are Indian women and Indian children in the welfare lines putting in full days in the endless round that is required to keep body and soul together if you need to justify yourself to the social workers and the welfare administrators. That's where the Indians who are not working are.

Please Parade Your Marketable Skills

Why aren't there Indians in the schools, teaching, or on the city council? Why aren't there natives on the police force or in the law offices? An on-going debate centres around whether the high rates of unemployment stem from native people being unprepared, uneducated, and unskilled, or whether they stem from natives being the victims of prejudice and discrimination. The truth, as always, lies somewhere in the middle. I visit a house in a northern suburb of Edmonton where four women are trainers in a federally sponsored program to enhance the employability of native women who have been on welfare. The program takes ten women for seven weeks, seven classes a year, and through a combination of classroom time and "work experience" with willing employers tries to funnel them into the active work world. The program teaches the women everything from grooming to coping with their children, filling out forms, opening their feelings to someone else when in difficulty, dealing with alcohol, and being more self-confident when dealing with employers and institutions. The trainers say all the things that I have heard before: the women are painfully backward and shy and are easily intimidated by employers, fellow workers, paperwork, institutions — anything. They have very low job skills and education. They sometimes have overwhelming personal problems that affect their employability. They have children who must be cared for; they have alcoholic spouses or men friends who beat them. They have debts. The women have drifted to the city often not knowing why; sometimes to pursue the bright lights, always because no matter how bad the city is, it is almost always better, more exciting, more convenient, with more opportunities than the reserve. The women have become dependent on welfare; their initiative is low. They almost invariably have a low opinion of their race and thus of themselves. Their image of Indians is little different from the worst image whites hold; lazy and drunk. Though they might separate themselves from the stereotype, it profoundly affects their sense of themselves in the world.

A native woman who is an employment counsellor at a Canada Employment Centre in Winnipeg summarizes her experiences in the following way: employers, she says, are frequently not willing to give Indians a chance. "I've had employers say; 'Don't send me any Indians'. Then I remind them that we have to abide by the human rights laws. Then they say; 'Yeah we know but we'll just say that they weren't suitable.'"

She says that competition for jobs is so intense that even the most menial job is sought vigorously. In such a world, given an unskilled Indian and an unskilled white, she feels that the unskilled white will almost always get the job. She says, as well, that employment counsellors will not antagonize employers by sending Indians to them if they know that they do not want Indians.

The same woman has worked as a teacher in Winnipeg inner-city schools. From her experience there she says that Indian people rarely aspire to jobs with status. Too many lack the self-confidence to think of themselves as policemen or nurses. Nobody ever told them as children to aspire to such roles in life. "When I taught in schools in the inner city," she continues, "the kids I taught would aspire to be waitresses or taxi drivers, nothing more."

A plethora of make-work and affirmative action programs have grown up in response to the unhappy employment situation of urban native people. Governments, of necessity, lead the way. A federal employment commission spokesman in Winnipeg pointed out that in late 1979 fully sixty per cent of the federal government's short-term make-work programs with ever-changing names like "Canada Works" and "Young Canada Works" were directed at native people. As well, the federal government has a low-level affirmative action hiring policy for its own staffs which at that time resulted, for instance, in five native employees on a staff of four hundred in the Canada Employment offices in Winnipeg. The government of Saskatchewan was more bold. Its resolution, with vague references to making its human rights legislation more persuasive, was to push in the early 1980s for ten per cent native quotas in all public and private employment in the province.

Accompanying these direct government efforts are a mixed bag of private agency enterprises usually financed by government monies. In Edmonton the Native Women's Employment Training program gently urges its charges off the welfare rolls and tries to find a slot for them in the work force. In Edmonton as well, a federally financed program called Native Outreach attempts to promote the training and hiring of native people in Alberta's burgeoning resource and industrial economy. Though George Arcand, a twenty-year-old Cree from a reserve near Edmonton, and director of field services, says that the program is actually rurally oriented and tries to give people work away from the cities, the Edmonton office has two counsellors who see seventy to one hundred people a month coming through looking for work in the city. The program tries to make training and apprenticeship arrangements, and lobbies with labour unions, government and industry for the hiring of greater numbers of native people.

An Outreach program in Regina operated by the Regina local of the Association of Métis and Non-Status Indians of Saskatchewan attempts to do the same thing; make arrangements for training and up-grading and lobby for hiring.

Amid all of these is an obsessive, almost mystical belief in "training", in taking "courses". Everybody is involved in a merry-go-round of courses that last from three weeks to several years in the complete accession to the maxim that the reasons Indians don't make it is because they have no education and no marketable skills. The quest for courses continues in a madcap, hungry sort of way; a mystic pursuit after some elusive Holy Grail. It would be fine if it wasn't for an underlying veneer of cynicism. The courses sell hope. But the hope is thin. And everybody knows this. Mabel Angelstad, the project manager for Native Women Employment Training in Edmonton admits that their success rate is one-third. That means that one out of three women who venture into the seven-week course will come out with her life noticeably changed; off the welfare rolls, capable and confident to make her own way. For the other two, it goes without saying; the experience will represent one more failure, one more hope cruelly shattered.

Both counsellors and students try to look away from the black hole of cynicism. They try to bounce back every time with a hopeful smile pasted firmly on their meet-the-public face. Native Women Employment Training say that they consider their thirty-three per cent success rate "pretty good". Native Outreach in Edmonton continues doggedly to cajole its people into courses so that they can get jobs with Esso Resources tearing up their homeland; they continue persistently to nurse their charges through their training, making sure they don't quit at the first sign of adversity. A Native Outreach worker in Regina talks bitterly about the racism of employers and the weaknesses in Saskatchewan's proposed affirmative action programs and then tells about sending two native workers through his service to a steel company. Each worker lasted only a half day before quitting. The counsellor says that

the steel company didn't call back for more help and admits ironically, "I guess all we can do is apologize and try to screen people a little better."

A field worker for a community college in Winnipeg tells about his tours through northern Manitoba, recruiting students for the mature student program at his college. The Department of Indian Affairs and the province of Manitoba provide grants to adult students to take a variety of training and trades. All the students in the program are native. The field worker says that no one has, as yet, graduated from the program that started in 1977, but of the fifteen who started then, only two are left. Everyone else has dropped out. They are pressured by the studying or by the city or by financial worries. They drop out for personal reasons or they start drinking or they get homesick. The two who still remain in the course are both women taking teacher training. Of the drop-outs, about half have remained in the city even though they have no jobs. Now the field worker is off on another trip north to find more bodies.

Repeatedly I encounter the admission that the training is not tough, not strenuous, not real. Almost everybody, particularly the Indians, says that a papered Indian is still less capable than a papered white. An Indian teacher in Winnipeg said she was glad she took her teacher training before a university in Manitoba set up a special section for training native teachers. She fears that her training would not have been as good nor would she be taken as seriously as a teacher. The courses, the training, the upgrading are seen as a sheltered workshop; the placements and the subsequent hiring are seen as being done cynically, for political, public relations or for charitable reasons.

This is the catch-22 of the whole employment conundrum. Nothing is ever seen as the "real world". Unemployment is so dismally high, its effects in poverty and dislocation are so much in the public eye, that governments are forced or embarrassed into redressive, stop-gap measures. But the redressive measures, instead of being temporary and a conduit into the wider world, too frequently become circular. No one gets out of the circle and the credibility of native people as workers is damaged still further.

The question "where are all the bus drivers?" remains an important one. For Indian people in the city it would seem that two things are important. One, critical to individuals, is having a job that is a source of income, a way to avoid the constantly threatening scourge of poverty and want. The other, for native people as a group, is having visible useful roles in helping make the urban community function. Too many Indian people are not employed at all in the cities. And those who are are too seldom seen; bus drivers, bank tellers, check-out clerks, policemen, doctors and nurses, cocktail waitresses. This is significant to the average white person on the street. He sees Indian people publicly in the unemployment lines or on skid row or as bureaucrats in the sheltered workshops of the Indian social welfare/political industry. He doesn't see Indian people as someone necessary to *his* daily survival, comfort and pleasure. He doesn't see Indian people as useful cogs in the daily on-going life of the city.

This seems to be one of the significant differences between the arrival of native people in the cities and the arrival of successive waves of foreign immigrants. For better or worse and for all their difficulties, immigrating groups in the past have been seen as necessary to the economy of the cities in which they arrived, if only, and this was certainly too often the case, because they would do the dirty work that no one else wanted to do. Indian people in the seventies and eighties have the misfortune of arriving into an urban economy that is already stretched thin; that is specialized and mechanized and that has little or no room for the unskilled or the untrained or the unsophisticated or anyone who does not buy wholesale the acquisitive, upwardly mobile values of the urban society. On all counts native people as a group lose. Too often and for too many reasons they are seen not as an asset to the urban economy but as a drain on it. They are the *lumpenproletariat*, always the surplus labour. Since as a group they are impoverished the urban economy can't even welcome them as consumers. They are the receivers of handouts, they are paid for non-production either through direct welfare or through subsidized training that goes nowhere, or through government make-work programs that are so ill-conceived, short term and cynically non-productive as to be pitiable. The whole situation is pitiable. It demolishes the hope and self-image of a whole generation of Indian people, and it locks the rest of the urban community into a bitter and condescending mindset.

A number of years ago, when black people in the United States were beginning to go through a not dissimilar adjustment to large cities, Daniel Patrick Moynihan, now United States senator from New York, advocated that the federal post office hire vast numbers of unemployed blacks to carry the mail. The implications were simple; a whole group of people who were hitherto involved in great economic and adjustment difficulties would be given dignified useful work performing a highly visible community service all the while marching proudly in the uniform of an agency of the United States government. While the same is not being advocated for the native people in the cities of western Canada, all discussions about employment have to lead to that place: the place of a paid and useful role, filled with self-respect and the respect of the community.

Three Men on Skid Row in Edmonton

On the downside of town, one week away from the wrecking ball, one step away from the bulldozer's blade, surrounded by the wreckage of a city in explosion, lie 96 and 97 streets. They snake around the eastern edge of downtown like an unwanted relative. Two streets lined with grimy hotels, cheap restaurants, rooming houses, pawn shops, and populated by a fringe of drunks and hookers, losers and n'er-do-wells.

In the early morning they gather for coffee in the front rooms of the social projects; the "happy gang", they call themselves, hung-over and in costume. One guy wears a T-shirt with "I am a wild Indian" lettered on the front of it. There is, at this hour, a lot of joking and laughter, a lot of kibbutzing with the woman behind the desk. There is quarrelling, the paying up of old debts, some scuffling on the street out front, some tentative entrances into the sexual dance. All waiting until 10:30 when the bars open.

Frank and David are brothers and come from Cold Lake, Alberta, 200 miles northeast of Edmonton. Frank is older, thirty-five, with long black hair, a linear face moulded around the broad bone of his forehead and high cheeks. He takes his wire-framed glasses off. Frank has a certain grace, a certain elegance and self-possession. He is worldly and he is sly. He sheds a tailored leather jacket and studiedly shows me the bear claw on a leather thong that he wears around his neck. He shows me a pocketful of wolf teeth that will make another necklace.

David is quiet. Black plastic-framed glasses keep slipping down his nose. His long black hair is braided. He is a small man, ten years younger than his brother. He wears a blue denim outfit, jeans and a jacket. He slouches in his chair when he sits, making him seem even smaller than he really is. He has no top teeth. He is just out of jail for reasons he won't tell me and I know better than to ask. I do know that he left Cold Lake under a cloud and that he feels that he cannot return there. He became an artist in prison and won a prize in a nation-wide contest for prisoner's art. He still draws pictures but doesn't sell many.

Ross is drunk. A Métis from Lac la Biche, he sits bleary-eyed, scar-faced, wearing a baseball cap and blue denim jacket. He tells me that he is just off work and hasn't slept yet. He also says that a trip to the bootleggers is all that is holding him over until the bars open in an hour and a half. Twelve years ago, when he was eighteen, he joined the army and went to West Germany as a paratrooper. He has been a drunk every since but still reads pocket books about the marines which he always carries with him.

David

I got seven brothers and five sisters. They're all scattered to the wind, gone in every direction. There's nobody back home. But I go up there every now and then. We stay out in the country as much as we can. Away from the noise and everything. It's deafening here, you know. You can't sleep, it gets on your nerves. If you don't sleep, you get depressed. You go out to the country to get a rest. When you're out there, there's nobody to get mad at, nobody to fight with but yourself.

Ross

It's one thing to go out there. But it's another to bide your time out there. You only live once. We're short enough now so you might as well enjoy it. You're going to go out anyway, it's a one-way ticket, that's all. My dad was just buried, what, twelve, thirteen days ago. I didn't even want to go to the funeral until the last twenty minutes, then I thought [Ross snaps his fingers] "let's go." My brother was waiting there, him and my other brother. I didn't want to go, I was in jeans and I had a western hat, a cowboy hat on, but I thought, "I'm going to go and make an appearance for the last time, pay my respects, what the hell." My wife was there and my little daughter too. But I told the old lady, "Don't ever cross my path again or I'll wipe ya" but I really appreciated her coming and showing her respects, I really did. It was a Legion funeral, my old man was in the Legion. But my cousin paid for everything, bought the old man some clothes.

I'm thirty-one, will be thirty-two. I was in the paratroopers, '66 to '69. I was in West Germany and western Europe. Did I get to see the world? Yeah. But I get to see the world right here, right here on Boyle Street!

Frank

I've seen the world too. Maybe it's okay if you're rich to go out and see the world. But it's not happiness. Happiness is a nice smile . . . feeling good . . . walking, seeing people . . . being able to live for something. Everybody's got something, a goal, something that makes them happy, it may not be very much. For some people it's a bottle of wine that'll make them happy. For some it's a nice looking girl with a nice smile. When she smiles at you, absolutely, I'm gone!

Ross

But if she's got a bottle, leave it there, I'll keep the bottle. [The three laugh together.]

Frank

I have sort of a plan, I want to do something, in that way I keep myself going. But for today I just live for it. If I do things good today, you know, you go down and you try to get a job or you try to get some money somehow . . . but I just live for one day at a time. Yesterday, I put it behind as the past, I don't drag it along. That way it's not very heavy. But if I drag ten, fifteen years on my shoulders, it's pretty damn heavy. So I leave yesterday behind. I've lived here on skid row, or in this part of town, for maybe twenty years. I was fifteen when I first came to the city.

Q. Where do you stay?

Frank

Oh we got a place to stay. We got a house, or we know some people, we got families here. . . . We got a place to stay. Let's put it that way. I don't stay in a hotel or in the hostel. I don't necessarily stay with people from my family. I could, you know, but . . .

David

I got friends all over. I got friends from the west coast right up to the east coast. And if I go to their place and I'm not too drunk or I present myself half decent, they let me stay, you know.

Ross

I got a trailer out in the country but when I'm in the city I stay in hotel rooms, it don't matter where. But today I never went to sleep yet. I been working at a job at a fertilizer plant, night shift. I just come back down here every morning. I'm a lancer. I use high pressure water to clean out these tanks at the plant.

But I stay in hotel rooms. I got relatives all over the city but I don't want to intrude on them. If they want to see me, they gotta come down here to the drag. Otherwise they won't see me. I won't call them. My old lady lives down there, my little daughter, I don't even phone them. They can come and see me.

If I want something, I'll go out and get it. I'm not a crook or nothing, I'll get it with my own money, my own determination, my own will. I don't need any of them although I do respect them for coming to my old man's funeral. Other than that I don't care if I ever see them again. Except for my little baby. She's going to have a birthday soon, she'll be six. So I'll send her a card, and a present, maybe twenty, thirty, forty dollars. Except I don't know what a little six-year-old would like.

David

I haven't been back to Cold Lake for about six years. Just recently I went back for a visit for about a week. But if people know your past, they tend to bring it up. It comes up at intervals, you know. But I don't let it bother me.

Frank

We get along okay here. That gang outside, those guys that call themselves the happy gang. I know them from around here from a long way back. We get along okay. I have a lot of laughs with them. They may not have much, you know, but I bet we have more than a million dollars of laughs. They get that sense of good humour even through all the hardship. They don't give a damn and nobody can

take that away from them. Some people when they get down here on skid row they end up at AHP, you know, down at Albert Hospital at the detox. They're not happy, they end up at the rehabilitation centre. But others stay here and they are happy because life is good to them, they live from day to day, minute to minute, drink to drink. I bet you any one of them if you ask them about dying, "Hey I never even thought of that," they would say. Drink to drink, make a few bucks.

Q: How do you make a few bucks?

Frank

Oh I have a trade, I can get a job. It's not hard. But the pay varies from maybe $3.50 to $11, $12, $15 an hour. You can be working for $3.50 and doing the same damn thing so they get you one way or another. After a while a guy gets sick of skid row and he's gone for maybe six, seven months. Out to work, out in the bush. And they live good when they come back, they got cash. A week and a half later they ain't got no cash!

Ross

There's a lot of Eskimos here too, you know, that we truck around with. They're good little people.

Frank

Us native people can live anywhere. We can live out there. Or we come in and we get the worst part of town. Why? It's a big why. Why should we live in a place like this that's got run-down houses and everything when we come to the city? Well maybe it's because that's the only place they'd rent us. I think that's one of the things. And then another is that nobody else wants to live here. Everybody else wants to live out in the suburbs. A lot of people come and they don't have that much cash with them and they take the first place they can get. If you want to rent a low-cost house in the suburbs you have to wait maybe a year. There's a waiting list must be from here down to Vancouver. So you can't wait that long, you've got to have a place right now. So you take the best place you can find and the cheapest. There's a place they call the reservation, just back here. And most of it is old buildings. There's quite a few natives live in there and around this district.

We don't have to live here, because there's millions of acres out there of beautiful forests and lakes. But we have to live here because you have to have cash. And this is the only place to get the cash and the jobs. Everybody moves toward where you can make a living.

David

I first came to Edmonton on my own when I was thirteen or fourteen because I thought the city was a place that was paved with gold. But I found out that it was a jungle where everybody was trying to step over the next person's head. If you live in a high rise, you got forty people living on top of your head.

Frank

I've lived in a high rise, on the twenty-seventh floor. When you get desperate, you live down here. I've lived down on the river bank too.

Ross

I left home when I was thirteen. My old man took me down to the road and gave me a kick in the ass and he said, "Okay, Ross, there's the road, truck her out." So I trucked around for a few years. I stayed with relatives here and there. Then when I was eighteen I joined the army. I signed up and I was gone. I went to Europe. When I got out, I worked around. I forged steel, and I worked at planers. I worked in B.C. for a while. Then I came back here to Edmonton. I got rolled here at the York Hotel, my whole paycheque from B.C. I had three tables goin', I was keeping them busy, eh? Then these guys rolled me and I got nothing. Money's no problem to me anyway. When I got it I spend it. Anyway I got rolled for whatever I had, I dunno, a few hundred. So the next few days I'm walking around and I got no money. These guys took me to the hostel to get a meal. I thought, "What kind of place are you taking me?" I looked ahead and there were three hundred guys in the line-up. My buddy in Germany had warned me, "Ross, don't ever get out of the army or you'll end up in the soup line." And there I was. I don't go there any more. I go out and work and get myself a hotel room, pick up some little broad. There's lots of girls around.

Q: Why do you come here to the Boyle Street Co-op?

Frank

I want to see the happy gang in the morning, first thing in the morning when they're alright. I don't like being around here in the afternoon. But I come to see who's around, see what you can pick up, maybe a smart saying, you know. Those guys out there are really good guys. If you get stuck, they don't care who you are, you could be the prime minister, and they'd put you up. These guys are alright. You give them a shave and give them some nice clothes and send them down to the Macdonald Hotel or to the Chateau Lacombe and they could sit there too. They're all human, eh?

The people who work here are A-1 too. They really care and nobody will lay a hand on them or else they've got to answer to the guys out front.

Where are the native organizations? Oh way down on the other side of town where no drunks come in! We go there too sometimes. They have a lot of services there. It's all native, Métis, and treaty there. They have good lunches there at dinnertime. A buck and a half.

There's quite a few agencies here in town where you can get casual labour; slave markets. You can get a few hours work, four or five bucks an hour. Mostly they send you to jobs that nobody else wants. Labour. Unloading boxcars or moving vans, maybe lancing oil tanks. What nobody else wants. That's what they give you at the casual offices. They open up at six o'clock in the morning, so if you're an early bird you can get out there and work. I went down there this morning at six o'clock. But we sat around for an hour and a half, a couple of hours, and nothing. I said "cut this" and left. There's a lot of work, but we come second, the Indians. It's not that we don't want to work, but we get discouraged, frustrated. So you walk into the first bar and sit down with whoever and order a couple. Then your wages go and you're worse off than ever. That's life.

I been living on skid row for two years. I come to this town to look for gold. And here I am.

I came here really, in the first place, to go to school. I was born in a log shack and lived with my parents and grandparents. And for the first seven years I spoke only my native tongue. Then they shipped me off to government residential school for twelve years. I prefer not to talk about that. It

was run by, what would you call them, a religious order of people. We had to go there and stay there and do whatever they told us. They were teaching us. Most of the time going to church and praying and saying poems, reciting nice little things about something that we didn't know. Something that happened overseas and we didn't know a damn thing about it. When I was done, I got the heck out of there. Then I went back to the reservation for a while. But they didn't have any higher education there. So I came to the city. And after a while I started looking around for excitement. I smoked a little dope. I didn't know there was anything wrong with it.

There were entertainment centres here but I was too shy to go into them so I would go with a few people instead and we would get a bottle of wine, go halfers, or split it a few ways. It didn't cost much. Then after we'd had the wine we'd go to the entertainment centres, dances, whatever they were and we'd look around for some girls. We began to know a lot of people. The other guys were hard-core guys. We'd get into some fights. Now when I look at it, many of those guys are gone, died, mostly through alcohol. Not many of them live long enough to die of old age. I'd come and go. I'd get sick of it and I'd go out of town and live with some relatives. Then I'd be back.

John, Regina

A large, burly, bear of a man, John sits solidly in his swivel chair talking about all the things he wants to do. The first thing he wants to do is join the RCMP. Ever since he was a little boy, he says, he has wanted to be a Mountie. He's about to realize his ambition by entering the training for special constables* six weeks after we talk. For this reason he is cautious about being interviewed. He doesn't want his full name used.

At present, John works for an agency in Regina that assists Indian people who are having problems with the law. He leans back in his chair. He speaks with the sureness and authority of a large man and a man with police ambitions.

He is direct. Fluent and sure of himself. He is a young man, twenty-seven. His mind is rattling with a hundred prematurely defined ambitions. He admits self-consciously after some time that he would ultimately like to become involved in politics, native politics, in Saskatchewan.

John has lived in Regina for many years, since he was fifteen. But he likes the country. With police work, he hopes to move to the country. When we finish talking on this day, he will leave for the country, to join his father taking some straw bales off land that his family owns seventy miles from Regina.

I'm a Cree Indian, I was born at the Piapot Indian Reserve thirty-six miles northeast of Regina. I lived there until I was twelve. Then I lived in Lumsden, Saskatchewan, where my dad worked on a potato farm. For many years we were constantly moving back and forth between Lumsden and Piapot as my dad worked with the seasons. My dad pretty well had to work out in order to make a living. It was through those times that I learned what I know about white society. That's why today I'm a pretty outspoken person because I grew up on the white side of things. Today, though, I'm proud of my culture and traditions which are Indian and I'm proud of my language, Cree, which I both speak and understand. But I got a very good idea of how to live with white people by living there; they were human beings too. Today I feel that I can cope with anybody. I feel that I gotta thank my father for taking me out and introducing me to that totally different environment. It's certainly helped me in what I do today.

I came to Regina with my family twelve years ago and found it totally different. All my older brothers and sisters were married at the time so I just came in with my younger sister and my mother and father. It was such a funny way how we came in; we had spent one night in town and we just decided that it was time to move in. I started working when we moved to Regina and I found once again that my experience living among white people had been very useful. In Regina my dad got a job with a hatchery and he worked there until he retired about six years ago.

At that time there weren't many Indian people in Regina. But just after that, about two years after that, it was just unbelievable the number of people who were moving in. All kinds of people were moving in from my reserve and others, mostly after the better jobs and with hopes of making good money.

It had been hard to make a good living out on the reserves. My brother, for instance, had tried to farm, but he had been pushed out by the big farmers. There are big farmers on the reserve but

*The special constable program was started by the RCMP to put native police in native communities. The special constables are just that, they are not members of the regular force.

since the space on the reserve is limited, the big farmers more or less conquer the little farmers. It was competition that was the big factor; small farmers like my brother just couldn't compete with the big farmers. He just had livestock and you can't make a living with just livestock. But he couldn't afford the big machinery that the big farmers had. Eventually he went into bankruptcy and after that he just fell apart. To be honest with you, where he is now, he's incarcerated. He got drinking and lost his driver's licence and one thing led to another. He just had too much frustration.

After coming to Regina I worked for a number of the native organizations such as the Métis society and the department of education. I also worked for my reserve as a recreation director. I didn't like working out there because although the money was good, you have to deal with all the internal politics. I'll tell you one thing about a reserve; if one family comes into power, it is all the members of that family that get the better jobs.

After my family moved to Regina, we'd have a lot of people, relatives and other people from Piapot who used to come and stay at our place when they came to the city. We have this idea that we like to help each other. We're that kind of a people. We don't like to see someone doing without something that we have. If we have something, we like to divide it in half . . . I guess that's always been part of our culture. This is in spite of the fact that in the politics on the reserve there is a lot of competition.

But people, close relatives and friends from the reserve, used our house as a shelter when they first moved in to the city. We gave them food, shelter, and the use of a telephone. A telephone was something that we had never had on the reserve. We had to sort of show them how to use it. When we came to Regina it was like we were right in the jungle. We were completely lost; we didn't know what to do. Then one family put us up for the night. It's funny how we do it, how we help each other. We may be losing that now. We may be losing some important things. I notice that Indians have always had respect, they've always respected their elders. We may be losing some of that now too.

My family still stays close to Piapot people. Every summer we go out there and that's where we have a reunion with our family. In the city we don't stay close in touch, I mean we don't see each other every day. When you first come into Regina you may want to keep in touch, but after a while you're going to want to have a life of your own. My circle of friends in Regina is the people I work with, the people from the project, people from some of the other offices that we work with, those are the people I associate with. And my family. I feel very close to my family.

I wish you could meet my dad. He had quite a life. He was the champion runner for all the Qu'Appelle Valley. He used to go into the marathons. He has a whole row of trophies and a book of clippings. He ran in the Boston Marathon once. Now he's seventy-three.

The work I'm doing now I see as a stepping stone to further work with the law. This is a real in-depth study, what I'm going through now, as far as I'm concerned. I'd like to become, in maybe eight or ten years from now, an Indian politician. I'd like to study some political science. I'm looking at the long term here. I'd like to see my people have a much stronger voice in the society.

I've always had a respect for the law and I've wanted to be a Mountie for about as long as I can remember. When I go into the Mounties this year I'll be a "special constable" and I'll do policing on reserves, I'll sort of be a liaison between the

Indians and the whites or the Mounties. That's a really good program, I think. When that program was started people didn't think too much of it. Now the native police are recognized as a necessity.

Here, working at this project we have authority, but not as much as we could have. When I go down into the police cells, there are some things I see that I don't like. I know that the officers have got to get their quotas. But it could be whites as well as Indians. I don't know how much of that I can change, I guess you'll have to interview me a year from now.

To be very honest with you, I have to say that I've lost a few friends since they heard it through the grapevine that I was going to become a Mountie. I lost a few. Some of them said; "You're going to be picking up your own people, don't you know that?" Or "You're going to be a flat-foot with your own people." Little cheap shots like that. Some of them call me a sell-out Indian but I know that they'd like to trade boots with me if they had a chance. I have to say that native people are really jealous people.

I know what I'm getting into. I've thought about it a lot. But it's a good career, I can do it. I know I can make a good Mountie.

I saw my first Mountie at a very early age. During Treaty Days when they came all dressed up to give out the treaty money. And then living at Lumsden; I had respect for the law from the time I was knee high. Now a lot of kids on the reserves, they don't see the police until they're maybe sixteen. That's too late. Too late to learn that they're there to protect as well as to enforce.

Urban Photographs by John Paskievich

Cops and Indians

I don't think most of our guys, the policemen, are familiar with the native culture, with their way of doing things. When they're out in the bush, they're used to just taking things when they need them; food and such is there for the taking. When they come to the city and do the same thing, they're locked up for stealing.

Winnipeg Police Inspector

Over the years there have been a lot of negative feelings, both ways, between the natives and the police. The police stereotype just like everybody else. Usually the only times that we meet native people, it's in an adversary situation. So the police start to think that all native people are like that.

Winnipeg Police Sergeant

Of the police in this city, eighty per cent are good men with wives and kids; they're trying to do an honourable job. Ten per cent would get their licks in if they knew they could get away with it. And the other ten per cent are rednecks. We try to get as thick a file as possible on these guys and maybe they'll get shifted to a paper-pushing job.

Director of Native Race Relations
Association in Regina

The native doesn't understand us at all, and we don't understand the native.

Regina Police Superintendent

Regina 1976

Most people will tell you with varying degrees of candour that in 1976 Regina, the Queen City, was on the verge of explosion. The city was fast developing the reputation as the meanest city in Canada for an Indian to live in. Perhaps not mean like a handful of smaller places scattered across the country where damaged Indians lie on the streets and open racial warfare is only the toss of a beer bottle away. But for any city of its size, large enough to qualify as an important Canadian city, Regina had troubles. Large numbers of Indians and Métis people, many of whom had only the slightest preparation for urban life, were moving into Regina. And since Regina was a small city — only 140,000 people — the Indians quickly became a very visible minority.

The Indians found life in the city difficult. And their presence made the white population increasingly nervous. Tensions and frustrations grew. Larger numbers of disoriented and poor native people congregated in the city's core. Many whites reacted badly. Downtown businessmen complained. The police started arresting more native people. Native anger and frustrations grew. A couple of downtown bars were torn apart in brawls. The native people became more and more angry with the police. The police were accused of being less than delicate in their handling of native people. An Indian woman's leg was allegedly caught and crushed in a police car door. Groups of Indian men and groups of off-duty policemen would reportedly wait around downtown itching for a confrontation. Five cases of alleged police brutality against native people were brought to the attention of the Saskatchewan Attorney General for investigation. It was deemed at the time that there was insufficient evidence to proceed with them. This didn't mollify the native groups.

It was at this time that native groups, civic groups, and the police came together to form the Regina Native Race Relations Association, the first of its kind in the country. It was hoped that the Association would at least lengthen the fuse on the situation. They hired a director — Fred Favel, a tough-talking Cree. He was asked to act on behalf of native people who had complaints about the police or who found difficulty with any aspect of the legal system; he would educate the police about cultural differences; and he would teach anyone in Regina who was willing to listen about the fragile balance of their city.

Winnipeg 1975

In October of 1975 the Institute of Urban Studies at the University of Winnipeg prepared a report for the Winnipeg Police Commission on the problems affecting law enforcement in the core area of that city. *Winnipeg's Core Area; An Assessment of Conditions Affecting Law Enforcement* was a weighty 140-page report that documented everything; housing, employment, schools, playgrounds, social services, and liquor outlets in an attempt to paint a picture of the inner city that would be relevant to decisions the commission had to make about policing the area. As well as chapters entitled "Conditions in the Core", "Crime in the Core Area", "Police Work in the Core", the report had an entire section on "Native People in the City". The inference was clear. Police work in the core of Winnipeg could not proceed without taking into account the presence of a significant group of native people.

The report pointed out that 37.8 per cent of crimes reported in Winnipeg originated in the core area, and that the percentage increased slightly to 39.6 per cent when crimes were weighed according to severity. It pointed out as well that the majority of the Indian and Métis population lived within the core area and constituted a majority of the clientele of such inner-city social services as the Main Street Project and the Salvation Army. These services described the native people who come through their doors as "lonely, defeated and unmotivated individuals." The police department told the surveyors that the percentage of native juveniles involved in crime was more a result of economic deprivation than of race, and the report quoted a Winnipeg judge, Ian Dubienski, who had discovered that native people in fact were involved in a low percentage of violent crimes and crimes against the person, crimes such as assault, wounding, murder, robbery, sexual offences, offensive weapons, abduction.

Native people most frequently ran up against the law, the study indicated, in the areas of liquor charges, prosecutions under the Child Welfare Act, and juvenile delinquency. Sixty-three per cent of charges against native people, said the report, were liquor charges; fifty-two per cent under the Intoxicated Person's Detention Act, and eleven per cent under the Liquor Act. Sixty-seven per cent of those charged in Winnipeg under the Child Welfare Act were native, as were 62.8 per cent of the juveniles encountered in the study's sample period, mostly for offences related to glue-sniffing and the consumption of alcohol by minors.

The report concluded that alcohol abuse among native adults and glue-sniffing among juveniles represented very serious problems indeed.

Native People & the Law:
A disturbing collision course

Statistics ought always to be treated cautiously. But what the statistics imply is increasingly disturbing; for native people, for police, for court officials. There is white man's law and there is Indian life, and the two do not have much in common. In fact, the white man's law and native people are increasingly in frustrating, paralyzing conflict. As native people move in larger numbers into the cities, this becomes more and more an agonizing fact of city life.

Studies of prison population statistics lead to horrendous conclusions. Visit any jail west of Sudbury and the conflict is made vividly graphic. Manitoba, which has a provincial population that is twelve per cent native, has a jail population that is thirty-seven per cent native at the federal Stoney Mountain Institution, fifty-six per cent native at the provincial Headingley Jail, and an astonishing eighty per cent native at the Portage la Prairie Correctional Centre for Women. Law Reform Commission of Canada figures show roughly similar percentages for other western provinces. Saskatchewan, with a provincial population that is just over twelve per cent native, has a prison population that is well over fifty per cent native. Alberta has a jail population that is more than twenty per cent native in its provincial institutions but a provincial population that is only five and a half per cent native. And in British Columbia, natives account for more than ten per cent of the prison population but only five per cent of the provincial population.

Theories about the conflict between native people and the law abound. None of them are in themselves adequate. There are the theories about "the white man's law" — the law which regulates and controls the native person's life but which is not based on his own culture or history and which does not reflect his values. These theories point out that the law is seen by the native as an enemy, not a friend. It is foreign to him; it always seems to be taking something away, be it his freedom or his money or his children.

There are other theories about conflict that result from an abiding and deep-seated bitterness. The native people, who, as a group, have endured brutal poverty, cultural dislocation, and the breakdown of their own family units through such things as the residential school system, are now so disoriented that they are unable to understand ways of functioning socially, and they are engaged in an ongoing, sporadic war of bitterness and rage against the white man and all he represents. There are theories that build on this; of sub-cultures of people who, when locked out of the dominant culture, take up allegiance with a culture in which success is measured by opposition to that which is important to the dominant culture, or by ability to annoy the dominant culture.

All the theories make a certain amount of sense individually and when individually applied. And yet each, by itself, oversimplifies an enormously complex situation. The issues between native people and the police or the law are the bottom line of all the accumulation of inter-cultural hurts and anxieties and grievances. The legal system has to react at the point where people start acting out individually and en masse, their frustrations; where they start actively hurting themselves and others.

The legal system and the police often react badly. The whole community reacts with paranoia, fear, and loathing. And the forces of law, as the experiences in Regina and in Winnipeg demonstrate, both reflect and compound this. The reaction is confused and it is severe.

The police forces, for the most part, have a methodical way of dealing with matters. Crime is crime. When there are more break-ins in one area of town, the police department increases its manpower in that area in order to apprehend and prevent. When there is an upsurge of street fighting at another corner, they do the same thing. They begin to notice patterns. A police spokesman in Regina says that as the population of native people in the city increased, the number of arrests for intoxication increased. The police also begin making general assumptions. A spokesman in Winnipeg speculated that the Indians must be moving from the Main Street strip, the skid row of hotels and cafes on north Main Street, to the burgeoning pin-ball parlour arcades on the north side of Portage Avenue, "Because there seems to be more trouble over there now." The police make some stabs at public relations; the force in Edmonton employs two native officers to burnish its image in the city's schools. But mostly they get caught up in the day-to-day clean-up and maintenance of the peace, and in responding to the fears of the community at large. And when they over react, or act badly, tension-filled situations like that in Regina develop quickly.

A Day in the Life of Fred Favel

The logo on the office wall is two hands, one white and one brown, inside a circle, reaching to clasp but not yet touching. They almost touch and yet they don't quite touch. The closed circle prevents them from escaping each other, giving hope that, in time, perhaps they will touch. It is a poignant, hopeful symbol; yet sharply realistic.

The office is in a little concrete block building on an industrial street north of the tracks from downtown Regina. Fred Favel sits limply in his three-piece suit behind the desk. He is tired. He wears a tight smile on an otherwise expressionless face. "One more time" he exhales. "That ought to have been our motto. Get 'em to give it one more chance." Favel is explaining about Race Relations, or, to give it its long form, the Regina Native Race Relations Association, of which he has been director since early 1978.

It is almost all he will talk about, and he will talk about it into the small hours of the morning when everyone around him is too weary to sit straight.

Favel is Cree. He was born in Winnipeg but has lived in Vancouver, Ottawa, and Montreal. In Vancouver he worked for the Native courtworker program and edited a newspaper called *The First Citizen*. He was an aide-de-camp to Alberta Indian leader Harold Cardinal, and in Ottawa and Montreal he worked as a journalist. Now he has been given the task of easing Regina's tense race situation.

He talks readily about himself. "It's entirely through a series of flukes," he says while sitting beneath a photograph of himself hobnobbing with Pierre Trudeau, "that I'm here working with the police trying to broaden their understanding instead of sitting in Stony Mountain Penitentiary after a total confrontation with them. I've been beaten up by police. I've been in jail. I've been through the Children's Aid thing. All of us have. I say there's a hairline between sitting here and being in jail. That's how close I am. Most people, unfortunately, are on the other side of the hairline."

Regina Native Race Relations Association was formed by native groups, civic groups, and the police in a desperate attempt to buy time to accommodate the burgeoning native population in the city. Three years is what it set out to buy. The project; with Favel, three caseworkers, and a secretary; is financed by the federal department of the solicitor general, the secretary of state department, the city of Regina, and a charitable foundation, the Donner Foundation. Its mandate is to act as an ombudsman between native people and the police, to function as an advocate for native people who are in difficulty with any part of the legal system, and to provide public education to the people of Regina about issues of race relations.

The docket at the police lock-up in the basement of the glistening new police headquarters in downtown Regina has thirty-seven names on this particular morning. They are arranged alphabetically, listed across from addresses, the names of arresting officers, and the charges. The charges range from being wanted on out-of-province warrants to theft, assault, driving while suspended, to a row of 106s — an overnight detention for being drunk with no additional charges laid. The three caseworkers pore over the docket. Seventy per cent of the names, they estimate, are native. When they visit the lock-up later in the morning, they will be given automatic access to the cells. They will interview the native detainees (and anyone else who might wish to see them) and they will provide a multitude of aids. They will call relatives to arrange for bail, they will call a lawyer, or a social worker, or they will take someone out in their own care. They may even represent an individual in court. They will help find jobs, help find social assistance, help prepare for a court appearance, interpret, and generally ease the complexity of bureaucracy. The three caseworkers do this every day, gaining their clients from the requests at the lock-up or from referrals from other social agencies, lawyers, police, probation officers.

The work the Race Relations Association does in representing native people in their complaints against the police seems to be having an effect. Up to October in 1979 there had been only three formal complaints laid against Regina policemen by native people. In 1978 there were twenty-eight.

Favel gives two reasons for the dramatic drop. Things have quieted down either because the police fear the public commotion that Race Relations could cause and so are more careful; or because police attitudes toward native people are genuinely changing due to the cross-cultural seminars conducted by Favel and his crew at police in-service workshops or at the police college. By having daily access to the cells at the lock-up, Race Relations workers are able to document situations as easily as the police can. This puts them in the position of being able to nip much trouble in the bud.

"We're usually satisfied with success through the back door," says Favel. "We'd rather work slowly. It's hard to make a complaint stick. The credibility of the complainant and any witness is usually impaired. Some people don't want to stick their necks out. The police have a strong union and can get good lawyers. If we get a high profile case, the media gets some sensational milage out of it, but you might win the battle and lose the war." Favel prefers to work quietly so that on the one hand the police know they are being watched and on the other Race Relations is doing work to increase cross-cultural awareness.

The Regina Native Race Relations Association also campaigns with the public at large. Favel claims he will go anywhere any time to talk about the race situation in Regina. And he does; from television programs to meetings of the Catholic Women's League. In each case he stresses how little time there is. He believes that when he took the job Regina had three years to turn matters around. When I talked to him, almost two-thirds of that time was up. His sense of urgency is only partly for effect. Regina, of any city in the country, has the most volatile race situation simply because of the magic of numbers; the native people are the largest and most visible racial minority. The gap of understanding between this large minority and the rest of the community is huge. To try to maintain peace between the native population and the police, believes Favel, would be only to deal with the symptoms of fear and misunderstanding, attitudes that are held by the whole community and which the police only reflect.

Favel believes that there is a significant difference that is cultural in origin in a native person's view of the law. "First of all," he says, "the law is viewed as 'white man's law'. Eighty per cent of the criminal code deals with property offences while many native people have no property to account for." Also, he says, the law with very few exceptions is written, interpreted by, and enforced by white men. So it is seen to be white law.

Native people, he continues, have a value conflict. The white law makes a difference between "law" and "justice". Or so the native person feels. "No matter what you've done, if you are white you get a good lawyer and you try to beat it." The law then seems to hinge on a good lawyer; pulling strings with powerful, well-connected people; making deals; looking for a technical out. "Native people," says Favel, "relate to none of these. If they know they are guilty, they become passive and accept what comes their way. If they are not guilty, they are still resigned to throwing themselves at the mercy of a system they don't trust and can't expect much from." If the native makes any aggressive motion toward the legal system, it is to run away. "Failure to appear is a huge problem with native people and the courts."

John Rockthunder, a Race Relations Association caseworker, puts it another way. "The thing you have to realize," he says, "is that the people we deal with are uneducated, unsophisticated, right out of the bush. Whatever jam they get into; trouble with the law, trouble with creditors; they react by getting passive, they just let it happen to them. They don't know who to turn to, so they don't turn to anyone."

Fred Favel contends that native-police relations are still a critical area to work on. "The only time native people see the police," he says, "is in a negative situation. The police don't come into the neighbourhood to buy the kids an ice cream cone or to talk about school or baseball. Every time you see a police car come into the neighbourhood, it means trouble." So he feels that there is a lot of work the association must do not only with the police, but with the Indian people to keep the channels open. But through it all he admits that it is a very thin line he and his co-workers walk. "We have to be very careful," he says, "that it doesn't seem that we are just making it easier for the justice system to process native people." The Race Relations Association walks this line delicately. If they do their job well, they know that they will be the darlings of no one. On the one side they attack a community's sins. On the other, they tell their own people not to give up faith. And they suffer for it. Some Indians, especially the more stridently political or the ones the project has not been able to be of any particular assistance to, see them as sell-outs; and they tell them so.

But Favel remains stubbornly optimistic; "I think that in a place like Regina the doors *have* quietly opened up. But too many native people have already said 'Piss on it, the society won't let us in.' The slogan of Race Relations should be 'one more time;' we're saying, 'give it another shot.'"

A Day in the Life of Dorothy Betz

It is nine o'clock on a Monday morning in a tiny office at the corner of the third floor of the Public Safety Building, the police headquarters, in downtown Winnipeg. The only window into this room, as in all rooms in this cold white fortress of a building, is a tiny slit high above our heads. Dorothy Betz is going over the court docket for the day with an assistant, Richard Cameron. Provincial Judge's Court meets in four courtrooms down the echoing hallway from this little office.

Dorothy and Richard read the names quickly and nod knowingly as familiar ones attract their attention. At one point Dorothy grimaces and bangs her head in mock despair against the top of her desk. She has come across the name of a young man who little more than a month before had been placed on probation — in her care. Now he is back in custody and on this morning's docket. She gets up from her desk and heads upstairs to the police cells. She's going to kick somebody in the ass, she says. Then she grins. And is gone.

Dorothy Betz is a Court Communicator in Winnipeg. A Saulteaux from the Pine Creek Reserve in northwest Manitoba, Mrs. Betz has been a court-worker with Indian people in Winnipeg since 1965 when she took on the job through the Friendship Centre. In 1971 the work she was doing was formalized under the provincial attorney general's department. Now she meets with native people who have been detained by the police, arranges legal assistance for them, interprets for them in court if necessary, and may end up, as with the fellow she will see this morning, taking them under her wing after sentence.

An enormously energetic and sympathetic woman, Dorothy, in her mid-fifties, will take her charges on as if they were members of a huge, endlessly extended family. By the sheer strength and effervescence of her personality she remains an island of warmth within the ice-scape of the criminal justice system in Winnipeg. She appears to take it personally each time one of her charges goes to jail. She remembers him and is always ready to go to court again when he comes back. And yet there is the tinge of despair.

Dorothy Betz will say quickly that Winnipeg is "not as bad as Regina"; which means that the situation between native people and the police in Winnipeg never reached the advanced state of open, outward, obvious hostility. Yet the difference is really one only of degree. And the difference may be one of sheer luck and timing. It is not because

Winnipeg has a corner on enlightenment that has eluded its neighbour city to the west. Or even that Winnipeg has tried harder. There is no obvious, visible reason why Regina should have gone to the brink and Winnipeg should have, up to this point at least, escaped such a fate. Fully half the names on the police docket this Monday morning in the Public Safety Building are native. The police know and predict that a majority of the calls they will answer on any given day or night in the inner city will involve Indian or Métis people. The police admit that they have no special understanding of the lives or the struggles of native people in the city. In fact, many officers will say that they find the whole issue exceedingly perplexing. Winnipeg has no reason to be smug. Winnipeg has every reason to struggle.

In small ways, the struggle is engaged. I travel one afternoon to a community centre in the north end of the city where twenty-two people from a variety of social agencies, government services, schools, and the police department hold a monthly meeting of a group called the Police and Natives Committee. Dorothy Betz has chaired this committee since 1975 when it was set up by the Chief of Police at the urgings of a city councillor. This day, as well as exchanging some information and perspectives about a recent craze for glue-sniffing by the area's teenagers, the committee discusses a paper that has been drawn up proposing a training in native culture for police recruits. If the proposal is accepted by this group and then, more importantly, by the city police department and its police college, the recruits who are about to enter Winnipeg's thousand-person police force would go through a series of seminars on such topics as; "A Comparison of Native and Euro-Canadian Values"; "Native Stereotypes, Prejudice and Discrimination"; "How to Relate and Interact with Native People"; "Factors which Contribute to Native Problems"; and "Re-

sources in the Community". The sessions would take up one and a half days of the recruits' thirteen weeks of training. The seminars would be given by Dorothy Betz and others like her from native organizations, social agencies, the university. It would be the first time anything of this kind has been undertaken with law enforcement personnel in Winnipeg.

Everyone at the meeting seems happy with the proposal. Someone asks if the same thing would be available through in-service training for present police personnel.

Questions about the law and native people can as easily be re-titled; "the dilemma of the police". Almost all comments about lack of understanding or lack of delicacy on the part of the police can be turned around to emphasize the essential perplexity urban police have in dealing with native people. The police see native people as a group of whom a large part live troubled lives and lives that are disoriented from the larger community around them. Critics wanting to make their point can say, for instance, "the Regina police are the worst in Canada". Or they can say, "the Regina police are in a difficult situation because they have to deal with the largest percentage native population in any city in Canada. And until recently, they attempted to do that with no training in dealing with people of native background and culture."

The police have the misfortune of having to come in at the tail end of a long series of other problems and misadventures. In Regina the police were the alleged villains. But the police protest that there is more to the story. There had been a history of troubles at liquor outlets. The police say that they would get calls to liquor outlets and arrive to find that there had been brawls and stabbings. The hotelmen and the downtown business people were upset. They were putting pressure on the police. The police were on the spot; they had to do something. There was enormous pressure on the police to "clean up" the downtown of Regina. So they started arresting many more Indian people. But a police spokesman says, "The Indians weren't the only ones to blame, because those same hotelmen still kept pouring the booze."

When the Regina Native Race Relations Association was formed, it was the police as much as any other organization who wanted to calm the situation, who wanted to have something that would take the pressure not only off the city, but off themselves. Regina Police Chief Al Huget went on the board of directors of the Race Relations Association. He gave its caseworkers ready access to the police cells; he welcomed cultural training for both his veterans and his recruits.

In Winnipeg, probably because the issue never developed as high a profile, the relationship between natives and the police was never considered independently in the same way that it had to be in Regina. Winnipeg, following the Institute of Urban Studies report in 1975, decided to address the policing needs of the urban core area as a whole, acknowledging, as did the report, that native people made up a significant part of the population of this core area.

The approach of the Winnipeg police became one that said; core problems and native problems are interchangeable. Many of the police calls are to low-income neighbourhoods in the inner city. It so happens that many of the inhabitants of these neighbourhoods are native. The same is the case on "the drag", Winnipeg's five-block skid row along Main Street. So no one will say if the issue for the police in Winnipeg is "native", or if it is "poverty". It was only very late in the game that discussions about cross-cultural training for police recruits in Winnipeg were undertaken.

Winnipeg reacted to the unique policing needs of the core area by instituting what it called Operation Affirmative Action (o.a.a.). This program took three districts in the core of the city and, in addition to regular police coverage, added sixty personnel under a full sergeant in each district to patrol on foot. The idea was not only to add police to a troubled area of the city, but to have the same police patrolling the same streets day after day; becoming familiar to residents, dropping in to the schools, the stores, the hotels, the social agencies, getting to know the area and the people. A police sergeant said, "The idea was to get the police to be more friendly, so we wouldn't have only the image of the authoritative type." The police department feels that it worked. Between 1976 (when o.a.a. was started) and 1979 the increase in the crime rate in areas where Operation Affirmative Action was in force was substantially less than the increase in the rest of the city.

In 1979, however, the program was cut back. City councillors from the suburbs started to complain that inner-city policing was causing their areas to be neglected at the same time as budget restraints prevented the police force from hiring additional personnel. So Operation Affirmative Action, though still maintained, was cut back as police staff were shifted around.

Neither Regina nor Winnipeg at this time employ native police officers. Neither city has made any specific attempts to recruit or train native police personnel though police department spokesmen in both cities hasten to offer that they "would be happy to employ persons of native ancestry if they met all the police department's existing criteria, and if they would apply". The police departments' existing criteria centre around size and weight specifications, academic qualifications, and the absence of a criminal record.

Actually, in the past both Regina and Winnipeg have had single native officers who came onto the forces through regular channels but whose careers were short-lived and unhappy. Their experiences were no more hopeful that that of an officer in Calgary. The city of Calgary, which in 1972 initiated a program to actively recruit native police, had its unhappy story recounted in the Institute of Urban Studies report. The Calgary police department launched a recruiting program and arranged with the Department of Indian Affairs and with Mount Royal Community College for upgrading and testing. One candidate out of five applicants was selected, completed a two-year police service course, and was taken on the force. Soon after this he "became intoxicated, pistol-whipped another Indian, was discharged from the force and was convicted of assault."

The consensus in the police department in Calgary was that the native constable felt pressure and hostility from his own people. He was under serious strain and he received little support or encouragement. Another Indian had failed.

These brief attempts and their concomitant failures seem to be evidence enough to urban police forces at the present time that programs of policing by natives, or any minority for that matter, are doomed to sorry ends. This is in spite of the attempts and the experiences of rural police forces across Canada, from the provincial police in Ontario and Quebec to the RCMP in western Canada, all of whom have reported on the desirability of providing a native component to police forces that operate on or near reserves or Indian or Métis or Inuit communities. And it is in spite of the very calculated thrust in numerous American cities to actively recruit and train police personnel from minority groups for work in areas of the city where those minority groups constitute significant parts of the population. One can hardly imagine a city in the United States without a black on its police force.

The Institute of Urban Studies report for Winnipeg advised that "the police not develop a special detachment of officers of native origin. But the police department should undertake a specific review of its overall manpower and recruitment training program with a view to enlisting members of different ethnic groups, in particular native people."

The recruitment and hiring of native police officers is not seen by anyone as a panacea for either the troubles of the native people or of the police departments. In fact the handful of native police in Calgary, in Regina, and in Winnipeg have encountered enough mistrust, skepticism, and outright hostility from their own people to frighten both other natives who would be police officers and native leaders. It is a vivid dramatization of the sorry state that now exists, a state in which the police are the most visible enemy of a group at loggerheads with the rest of the community. If a native person joins the police force — the enemy — he or she has not only sold out and gone over to the other side, but has become a tool of the other side's oppression.

This unfortunate state of affairs must be addressed by both police and natives in the next decade. The same can be said of the police as was said of schools and teachers; as long as they are seen as the enemy, the mistrust will be huge and so will the grief.

Colleen Morriseau, Winnipeg

Except for a brief period when she attended university in Brandon, Manitoba, Colleen Morriseau has always lived in Winnipeg. She was born in Winnipeg. But she was seventeen years old before she met and became friends with any other Indian people. Colleen Morriseau was given up at birth by her Indian mother and was raised by white parents in a foster home in an all-white suburb of the city. She went to all-white elementary and high schools. She knew that her colour made her different and she suffered her share of taunting because of it. But she didn't understand why.

When she was seventeen and first met other Indian young people all sorts of unexplained things about her life started falling into place, "Everything exploded for me," she says. She went through a painful and exciting six years of discovering a new self, of learning about the heritage of her race, of living through a period of pain and guilt and ultimately of reassurance with her foster family. Now, at twenty-five, she is settling into her adult life. She has just completed her B.A. at the University of Manitoba and she is looking for permanent work in some field that would have to do with the lives of native people.

I was born in Winnipeg. I was taken into a foster family, never adopted, but taken into a foster family. I grew up in East Kildonan which is a suburb of Winnipeg. When I was growing up, in the sixties, I was the only Indian child in my family, in my neighbourhood, in my school. I felt that had a big effect on me. It was very difficult for me. I was very shy and still haven't gained a lot of self-confidence though I have a lot more than I used to have. I found when I was going to school that some of the kids were really mean to anybody who didn't fit. Even if you were fat or if you wore glasses they picked on you. To me they used to say that I was dirty, that I shouldn't be there, why didn't I go back to the reservation? They would ask who did I scalp last night. I'd say "Why do you ask me those questions? I'm not like what you read in a book." And I'd have to go home and ask my mom, "Why do they ask me those questions?" And she didn't know the answers. All she could say was that they didn't know enough, they're ignorant. I guess I grew up around a lot of people who didn't know or understand and so I always had to wonder.

I guess the kids got their ideas at home, what they heard about Indians and what they saw on TV in John Wayne movies. You know, riding horses and scalping people and making a bunch of noises when we attacked. Also the adults in that neighbourhood weren't very open. My parents had decided that they would accept me but they were never sure how anybody else would accept me. They said that they found out who their real friends were when they took in an Indian foster child. Some of the people in the neighbourhood didn't talk to them after that. They were left out of things, neighbourhood parties and so on. That had an effect on me. I always felt that whatever happened to them, it was my fault.

There were times when my mother would be visiting the neighbours and I would go to look for her and the neighbours would send me home to wait for her while the other little kids would be inside waiting for their mothers. One time when a neighbour did that, sent me home to wait for my mother while the other kids were inside, my mother left and never went back there again. I think they went through just as much as I did at that time, in the early sixties.

At school I remember getting terribly embarrassed when they talked about Indian massacres and savages. My worst experience was in grade four when they were talking about massacres and one of the kids put up his hand and asked if any of my family had been involved in these massacres. I started to cry and I wanted to go home right away. Once they asked me if I had ever been to a massacre. Or they asked if we had scalps at the reserve. I think it's better now, they're learning about the different Indian cultures, the plains culture, the B.C. culture. Indians were just Indians when I went to school.

I didn't deal with all this very well as a child. I became very introverted and I wouldn't talk to anyone. I just stayed away, I avoided questions and I avoided everybody's eyes. I just didn't want to have them bother me anymore, I just wanted to stay by myself. Even when I finally went home I stayed in my bedroom and I played by myself and I did things by myself. I wouldn't go to call on anybody because I didn't think they would want to play with me. I'd wait until they'd call on me. It would take a lot of courage for me to go and call on anybody. I'd build up all these things in my mind, that I'd call up this girl and what would she say. But when I finally did call it would never be as bad as I thought it was going to be. I built up this worry and insecurity in my mind.

At home I saw a lot of my parents speaking up for me and defending me, at school, with the kids. If the other kids would hit me with their sticks my mother or my father would come out and tell them to go home. I never had the courage to stand up and fight for myself. They were doing all these things for me and when the time came to do them for myself, I couldn't. I was scared to speak up for myself until much later. But now I learn that other native kids are going through it much later.

They're going through now what I went through ten years ago.

For a while my parents thought that if there was another Indian child around it might be better for me, that I shouldn't be by myself so much. So they arranged with Children's Aid for my brother who was a little older than me but was also in the city to come and live with us. But it was even more difficult for him. He was always getting into fights. It was never very easy for him.

The first time I asked, "What am I, what nationality am I?" because I had noticed that everyone else around me had blond hair and blue eyes, or brown hair, my mother sat down and told me that they had adopted me. They told me that right from the beginning. And she told me that I was an Indian person though they didn't have too much of my background from Children's Aid. They told me what they could and what they had learned. They told me that they always had a lot of questions about taking me but that they were all for my sake, whether it would be the right thing to do for me. They felt that they should take me but they always had questions about whether they did the right thing, right up to today. I still have to tell them, "Yes, you did the right thing."

I finally learned a little about my real mother and father. I heard that they were alcoholics and that they separated while my mother was carrying me. After I was born she went to Toronto. I could have had a chance to meet her a couple of years ago but I didn't. Not because I hate her or anything, but the past is the past.

When I was seventeen I met my first other native person outside my family, and through that person and a couple of others I met this man who I eventually married. These people were into the native cultural thing at that time, in 1972, and they were going to the Winnipeg Native Club where they had pow wows every Thursday night. The first time I went to a pow wow I couldn't believe it. There were so many Indians there. I felt uncomfortable at first but then I really got into it. There was so much I wanted to learn, I started going to every pow wow I could find. I started talking to elders, I started growing my hair long and braiding it. I started going out to the reserve at Fort Alex. It was very exciting. It was almost as if I had to prove to myself that I was an Indian and that I wasn't ashamed any more. I was doing all these things; I joined a pow wow group, I went to a sundance, I started reading all these books. I got involved in feasts, I learned to cook rabbit, I learned how to cook bannock. It was just so many things. I was just fascinated by the whole thing.

This was difficult for my family because I was wearing beads and feathers and braiding my hair and going out. My mom was interested, she wanted to learn what I was learning. But she always seemed to want to apologize to me for not teaching me these things. And I think she felt a bit guilty. But it also brought us together because I was telling her what I was learning and so she was learning too. She had always told me that I was an Indian and that I should be proud of that. But she also told me that she didn't know where I would get support for that; she knew that she couldn't support me in my culture. But now she seemed happy that I was finally finding myself. She had always been worried about how I would find my way.

Now I think I could live in two worlds if I had to. I could take a job and live in a non-native community, I could handle it if they were racist or prejudiced. I could also live in a native community and be accepted on a reserve. I can live in the city and be accepted on a reserve. I can go to the Northstar Inn or I can go to a pow wow or I can go to a reserve and I can have a good time at all of them. And there aren't many people who have had those kinds of experiences. When I couldn't find a job in September I had to go to the city welfare and I was sitting there when all these things came to me; I've been to the Northstar Inn and I've been to city welfare!

I was lucky to go through all of that back then. My sister is now twenty-eight and she is going through what I went through when I was seventeen. She's going to every pow wow now, she's growing her hair, she's going through that whole identity thing. She grew up with a family that was French and they never encouraged her to learn anything about herself and she's just learning all of this now. She was quite comfortable up until she was twenty-five, she wasn't looking for a native identity at all. Then I took her to a social and she started experiencing all the things that I had felt.

I still feel that I have to go to pow wows and ceremonies both for the social part of them and for the support to my own identity. It's hard to put it into words. But whenever there's a pow wow, I always go. It's something I find that I can't keep myself away from. If there's a feast or celebration at the Friendship Centre or Indian Days or Treaty Days out at the reserve, I will go. I need those things to do what I have to do during the rest of the week. I don't write to elders or seek them out. If they are there I'll go and talk to them but that's about it. There are some elders who will interpret your dreams for you but I haven't done anything like that. It's reassuring to know that they are there. I just like to hear them speak. Hearing them speak is something that is important to me even if I don't talk to them.

My years in university were very exciting. I was really taken by the interest in native studies at the universities. In Brandon they had set up special programs for natives. It helped native students. There was a native support group that I knew I could go to if I needed to, I learned a lot more about native peoples at university, their histories and their migrations. It gave me a broader view. Not just culture and not just religion. I learned about politics and economics, Indian alliances, Indian social economics, trade. It was a very interesting experience, university.

I've had some difficulties. I only stayed one year at the university in Brandon. My marriage broke up then. We were married for two years but I guess my husband was an alcoholic. He was a binge drinker. He'd go away and not come back for three days. After two years I couldn't take it any more. So I came back to Winnipeg and finished university here. But even though it turned out bad he was the one who introduced me to a lot of cultural things that are very important to me.

There are still times, too, when I get insecure and think I'm being discriminated against. When I'm in a store and they take a long time to serve me or they are impolite, the first thing that still jumps into my mind is that they are prejudiced against me. Even if they are not. A white person would just say, "Oh she's really in a bad mood today," but a native worries that it is because they are prejudiced. I remember once in Eaton's I wanted to buy a pair of gloves and I was standing there for the longest time and nobody would serve me, they kept walking past me and I was standing there with these gloves. I finally got so angry that I just took the gloves and walked out of the store. And nobody stopped me. When I got outside I suddenly realized what I had done.

What I'd really like to do is write, maybe go into journalism. I'm really interested in native history and in getting the oral histories validated.

Legends and myths, I'd like to see that. Or I'd like to work to revise some of the textbooks I had to learn from in school when I was a kid and change all the things that just weren't right. I haven't looked into that, but I'm just thinking of what I would like to do. Or maybe I'd like to work in something in education, developing a native history course or native social studies. Something that would show us in a more positive way. Because we're always seen in the negative, defending ourselves.

I think as far as the future is concerned, I can be most useful in the city. I don't really know the language well enough to work on reserves. I speak English much better than I do Cree or Ojibway. So I think I could work better in the city community. I feel I am a city person, although I'm not sure because I've never really lived on a reserve. So it's hard to say.

The Dilemma of the Social Services

Edmonton

According to its director, Alice Hansen, eighty to ninety per cent of the people who come through the doors of the Boyle Street Co-op in Edmonton "look native".

The Boyle Street Co-op is on two floors of a run-down building on 96 Street. Out front, on a sidewalk littered with broken glass and the hopeful pokings of creeping weeds, are five drunks — three girls and a couple of young men, one in an absurdly large cowboy hat — involved in a little square dance that abruptly turns into a quarrel. I squeeze past them and through the wooden door into the dingy orange reception room. A rheumy-eyed young woman approaches me, stepping over the encasted leg of a man with crutches who is asleep, his head resting on the phone book on the reception desk beside him.

The Boyle Street Co-op is a collection of social services all under one roof. Like a social-work smorgasboard, it offers a drop-in centre, advice and aid with housing problems, aid in finding employment, counselling, and assistance of any kind from filling out forms to commandeering prompt medical attention. The co-op has been in existence since 1973, a project of the Preventative Social Services division of the Alberta Department of Social Services and Community Health with co-financing by the city of Edmonton.

The neighbourhood surrounding the Boyle Street Co-op isn't *on* the downside of town, it *is* the downside of town. Across the street is a sizable skid-row hotel. Just a stone's throw away are nine more. To the south and around the corner is the Salvation Army's Men's Hostel. Within a half-dozen blocks are a collection of flophouses, rooming houses, pawn shops, laundromats, greasy spoon restaurants, and the occasional meticulously kept home of a pensioner or a Chinese family.

It is a neighbourhood of chaos and tears and assorted human tragedies dragging themselves from one crisis to the next in a series of hopeful, halting, painful, agonizing gestures; futile graspings at the elusive bobbing duck of life. It is also a neighbourhood of special joys and moments of spontaneous laughter. But mostly it is a neighbourhood of hurt and self-immolation with residents too damaged to function or even to care anymore.

It is a bittersweet, tough area of town to live in. And as tough an area to work in. The social workers at the Boyle Street Co-op care about what they do, about the assorted casualties who stream though their doors. And yet they have to make jokes with each other in order to survive. There is a tentative trust between them and the skid-row people who frequent their offices. There are unwritten rules that each live by in order to survive; the unspoken agreements on how far each goes, the shrugged-off disappointments, the stamina to try again. The workers are honest, sincere, pained people; Danielle, pretty in a bruised-at-the-edges kind of way, who came looking for help and came back to work; Mary, with a Mother Earth capacity to enfold and care; Alice, who left the suburbs to work on 96 Street, and who now runs the project and chases the city for money.

We repair to a back room to sit around a long table sharing a litany of personal frustrations; a worker spent a day walking the streets trying to find someone to rent a room to a homeless drifter only to get a call a week later from the landlord complaining that twelve people have moved in so he is evicting everyone; another worker day after day, week after week, journeys through the halls and corridors and administrative offices of schools and hospitals and other institutions accompanying and speaking for young women and their children, struck dumb in terror by crisp offices and officers and paperwork.

The frustrations are the very human, front-line frustrations of people who daily work on the streets and the neighbourhoods with individuals whose lives are in chaos, leading them by the hand through the intricate maze of forbidding bureaucracies, terrors, and pitfalls in search of a day's work here, a place to live there, some legal help over here, some clothes for the children over there, a chance to sober up, an admission to hospital. It goes on. The workers complain that it never ends. Every morning is the same. Possibly not the same casualties as yesterday morning, but the same kinds of casualties and just as many. It never seems to get better.

Regina

Ed Kempling is a tall rambling man in his mid-fifties. A United Church minister by profession, he has been, since early 1978, the co-ordinator and sole employee of that church's Native Concerns Committee in Regina. He works out of a cluttered, wallboard-panelled office in a building near the tracks in the heart of the city. The building also houses the Native Friendship Centre and an assortment of small Indian bureaucracies. Kempling has spent most of his adult life working with native people. He worked early as a residential school principal in Alberta and on Vancouver Island. He is an intriguing figure really. He embodies many of the paradoxes of the times. His favourite story is about a church in Hamilton, Ontario, which, having a load of used clothing to give away, put it on a truck and sent it north to the Cape Croker Indian Reserve at the base of Ontario's Bruce Peninsula. When the truck arrived, the driver took it to the chief's house and asked what to do with it. Without the slightest bat of an eye, the chief calmly directed the driver to a cliff that spilled out over Georgian Bay and told him to dump the load there. That, he said, is where they put their garbage. Whether or not they needed the clothing was irrelevant to the chief. What he wanted to stop was the uninvited charity.

Kempling likes to recount the story and has tried to learn his lesson from it. But its truth hasn't made his job any easier. The story, for him, represents a watershed in the relationship between native people and the churches in Canada. Kempling talks about being at the tail end of the missionary mentality. He talks ruefully about "bodysnatching trips" he made in the 1950s to bring children back to his school. He hastens to add that it seemed the right thing to do at the time.

The Native Concerns Committee is over twenty years old. It started out in the late 1950s by rescuing young Indian girls fresh to the city from ravishment at the hands of unscrupulous skid-row types. The committee put the young girls up in rooms and gave them the assorted necessities of life. But then city welfare organizations and eventually native organizations started doing the same things. Not only did the native organizations do them well, but they began to insist that they and they alone should do them. This left operations like the Native Concerns Committee and their staff with an identity crisis.

In a way the whole Christian church shares the identity crisis. On the one hand it has for so long lived with the impulse to "do good", whatever in the end that might have turned out to be, and now it finds that impulse stymied by the new assertiveness of the native organizations. On the other hand the churches are afflicted with a growing and potentially paralyzing prepossession with liberal guilt.

Ed Kempling seems caught in the middle, in a sense too smart for his church at both its extremes. He resists the missionary impulse, the people who keep asking him why he doesn't start an Indian congregation, as simplistic. And he seems embarrassed by guilt-inspired breast-beating. Instead he wraps himself in information. His desk is littered with studies and charts and proposals. He lugs around reams of statistical data and newsprint charted in felt marker which he tapes to the walls in church basements and from which he tries earnestly and sensibly to define ever more clearly the Indian problem. He is at pains to explain to his now all-white audiences how infinitely complex the situation of native people has become.

Winnipeg

Alan Howison is worried. "We know," he says, "that a heavy proportion of the dislocated people in our community are native." He is speaking of Winnipeg. "We *know* that," he says once more for emphasis. He lists the names of some treatment centres for adolescents and points out that at least half the population of those places, for example, is native. Howison does not work for a social agency. But as executive director of the Winnipeg Foundation, one of the oldest community foundations in the country, he helps finance many of Winnipeg's services and agencies. Across his broad walnut desk comes a veritable parade of proposals and requests for money, all of which emphasize the needs of dislocated native people. Whether it's an agency dealing with ex-convicts or a city hospital wanting interpreters for patients who speak only Indian languages, the cry for services for native people and for money for those services is never-ending.

The community, acknowledges Howison, (whose foundation gives out a million and a quarter dollars a year), is willing to spend money and energy in this area. But it is frustrated at seeing its money going to make-work projects that don't go anywhere, that don't turn into real work.

Howison himself is a great fan of what he calls the multi-service approach. He is weary of a dozen different social workers and social agencies all operating on a single individual or single family like so many sub-contractors in the auto industry. Each service takes a piece, be it medical or legal or correctional or financial or psychiatric, until the poor subject is torn in too many ways to know what is happening. By virtue of inter-agency rivalries or statutory jurisdictions, there is scant, if any, communication or co-ordination between services. And the cumulative price tag for their efforts is staggering. He believes that the record in Winnipeg is twenty-two agencies all working simultaneously with one family.

Better, argues Howison, to bite the bullet and say that for certain sorts of disfunctioning families the treatment has to be different. And then have some government take the initiative to make sure that some sort of co-ordination is legislated and adhered to.

Keeping the Lid On

The first thing to remember when discussing the social services, as with housing and employment and law enforcement, is that their use is ensured by a person's poverty, not by his race. As a social planner in Winnipeg put it, "poor people get sick more, are unemployed more frequently, have more problems with alcohol and with the police and whatever else comes under the list of social services." If native people are seen as a load on the urban social services, as they frequently are, it is not because they are native, but because they are poor. Native people in cities are more frequently poor, and they may be poor *because* they are native people, but that is another question.

The other thing to remember is that the social services don't change things; they merely keep the lid on. In Edmonton, one worker on 96 Street lamented that the "system" he worked in wasn't geared to prevention, in spite of the words they used, just to treatment. It's ironic that he should find this surprising. In Winnipeg, Tim Sale, the executive director of that city's Social Planning Council says; "What most people don't understand is that the social services are systems of control and support, not of change. They ameliorate problems, they don't solve them."

Almost every urban social service, those helping professions from welfare workers to medical services to counselling services to children's aid to group and treatment centres for delinquents to skid-row hostels and street workers, will say that the influx of native people to the cities has put a burden on their service, that native people have become a substantial part of their particular case loads. The director of a skid-row drop-in centre in Winnipeg that provides a floor to sleep on overnight for those too drunk to go home or get into the Salvation Army hostel, and that provides a detoxification centre for those in even worse shape, claims that ninety-nine per cent of his clients are native. The same is the story with only some variance in numbers, of welfare-case workers, probation officers, inner-city health centres. The agencies that keep statistics are ready to trot them out to underline the argument. Those that don't are willing to speculate to draw the same conclusion.

Furthermore, costs are cited that are horrifying to say the least. In a 1976 study for the government of Manitoba, social anthropologist Clement Blakeslee startled provincial legislators by speculating that:

> The average Indian consumes medical and hospital services at two and one-half times the provincial average...welfare costs for status Indians run many times higher than is true for the average Manitoban...the average cost of education for a status Indian is about twice that for the general population....Corrections; jails, police, courts and related services cost on behalf of the average native person nearly as much as health services or educational services.

Tim Sale says, "yes, the figures are not difficult to believe." But he stresses that that is the case with all poor people; all poor people consume those services at gluttonous rates and if there is a disproportion for the average of native people, it only serves to demonstrate that the average of native poverty is that much higher than in the society as a whole.

The $130,000 Family

In 1979 the Social Planning Council of Winnipeg decided to tally the treatment and care-taking costs of one family. It was a large family; a man, his wife, seven children. The children ranged from the cradle to young adulthood. It was also a "multi-problem" family. The father and an older son were in jail. Two children were in treatment homes. Another child

was a regular with the school psychologist. The mother and the remaining children were on welfare. The planning council used only the identifiable direct costs in making its calculations. They knew, for instance, that the annual cost of keeping a man in a federal prison at the time was $20,000. And they knew that the cost in a provincial jail at the time was $15,000. They knew the daily cost per resident at the treatment home for adolescents was $100. They knew what the school psychologist's time was worth, and they knew how much the mother at home was receiving in welfare.

They didn't calculate the time and expenses of the welfare worker or the welfare department bureaucracy. Nor did they calculate the court and police costs or a host of other possible expenses that are almost impossible to add up but are there nonetheless. Still, the bill for this family came to an astonishing $130,000 for the year. And the family remained "bone poor".

Tim Sale suggests that this family would be at the upper end of the costly families, but estimates that there might be five to seven hundred multi-problem families in Winnipeg for whom somewhat similar calculations could be made. Alan Howison, speculating on the same problem says, "I'm only guessing, but I think you'll find that those hundred-thousand-dollar families are more common than you'd dare dream.

The horrors that these costs conjure up are more to be blamed on the social service system, the social service industry, than on the persons and families on whom they are spent. It defies the common man's imagination as to what sort of care and assistance and treatment can possibly cost the public $130,000 a year and still leave a family toward whom it's supposedly all directed in abject poverty and anger and despondency. Yet it apparently happens every day. The social services, with few exceptions, are shamelessly unrepentant. Indeed, they protest that they work hard and with sincerity. In most cases they certainly do. Then what is wrong?

Those who advocate the multi-service approach argue that "fragmentation" is what is wrong. They can list the twenty-two agencies at work with one family as did Alan Howison, and can argue quite persuasively that one worker with a much broader jurisdiction would be more effective — and less expensive. But at the present time we are stuck with many services, each justifying its existence by grabbing a piece of the human problem. Health is health and welfare is welfare and children's aid is children's aid and corrections is corrections and education is education and psychiatry is psychiatry and so on. Never the twain shall meet. Some services are municipally financed, some provincially, some jointly. Some, particularly those dealing with status Indian people, are federal responsibilities.

In Alberta the provincial Department of Social Services and Community Health finances social services through three divisions, usually with cost-sharing by the city. Welfare is provided through the Public Assistance Division; family intervention is undertaken through the Child Protection Division; and financing for special projects like the Boyle Street Co-op is given through the Preventative Social Services Division. But if you are a status Indian in Alberta, or anywhere in Canada, health, education, and welfare benefits come from the federal Department of Indian Affairs. That is, they do until you have been off the reserve long enough for your status to get murky; then the squabbles between provincial and federal governments about whose responsibility is what really start.

Besides that, the army of private agencies dealing with native people may get their support federally, from the department of the Secretary of State or the Canada Employment and Immigration Commission, or the solicitor general. Or they may get it provincially, in Alberta from one of the divisions of the Department of Social Services and Community Health. If this doesn't complicate things enough, the Alberta government is setting up a provincial Native Secretariat whose programs, it is predicted at this writing, will be financed by provincial funds but will be the administrative responsibility of municipalities.

One former employee of the Department of Social Services and Community Health who preferred to remain nameless said that, "When an Indian comes to town needing assistance, with housing or employment or welfare or whatever, the practice was, if they were treaty, to send them to Indian Affairs. In turn, Indian Affairs sent them back to the reserve. It wasn't the stated policy, but that is what happened."

The dilemma in the social services isn't only over costs and jurisdiction. The dilemma or the frustration is mainly that of a society that doesn't know how to help. In Edmonton Alice Hansen talked about the regulars who appear daily in her doorway and commented that native people become very dependent on things like the social services and on the city welfare system because they are coming from the dependency of three generations of a reserve culture. The frustrations of some of the workers I talked to in Edmonton were the frustrations of people who can't get away from those they are trying to help. Life is brightened by the rare moment when someone they have worked with ventures out independently. But they wait in vain for the city around them to become a more hospitable place. And they too often arrive in the morning to find yesterday's or last week's or last month's client waiting in the same condition on the same step for the same assistance. A native woman in Winnipeg who has worked for many years in the social services is fond of saying that you can counsel an alcoholic or a criminal or an unemployed person to death, but the only real change comes the day they go out to get a job by themselves.

Institutions share the dilemma. Ed Kempling in Regina has realized (and now must persuade his church) that the church's tradition of charity has seen its day. If institutions like the churches are to be of any use to native people in the cities, it is not by giving them what they can get for themselves, but by setting the church's own house in order so that at least one part of the urban society is willing and ready to move over to provide room for the native. It is a hard realization to come to. But it is the one that to Kempling makes the most sense. His "clientele" now, if that word can still be used, is not Indian people at all, but middle class whites in their church pews.

The social services will change. They must still provide aid for poverty-stricken and disoriented groups of people who arrive on the city's doorstep. They must still be prepared to deal with children from chaotic homes; they must still ensure that the necessities of life get distributed to persons and families who have none of them. And they must still give counsel and aid to persons whose lives are in turmoil. But they must do those things without creating the appalling dependency that is witnessed all around now. They must do them and, like Ed Kempling, be prepared to stop doing them when they are no longer needed or when people can do them better for themselves. They must do them without the happy, boundless budgets most jurisdictions enjoyed through the 1960s and most of the 1970s. And, last of a tall order, they must do them amid the growing, and in some quarters near rampant, skepticism that their efforts evoke from the public at large.

To clarify their perspectives in their relations with native people, there are some key questions that the social services, of all elements of the community, must address. The questions are borrowed from the writings of William Ryan in a book, *Blaming the Victim*, (Random House, 1971) about social work with minority groups (blacks and Puerto Ricans) in American cities.

The theories around "blaming the victim" presuppose that the subject, or client, of a service is both a deviant from some preordained norm that he has no right to deviate from, and that he somehow is in control of his circumstances to the extent that his deviation is a kind of perversity that he chooses quite consciously to inflict on the society around him. With those beliefs it is easy to choose psychology, for example, or home environment, or diet as the culprit if a child is not doing well at school. The fault is not with the school because it, after all, represents the norm that the child ought to be adhering to. The same tricks can be turned around questions of work habits, social behaviour, the raising of children. The list can go on.

Ryan suggests that for people in the social, medical, educational, and psychological services who work with a disadvantaged group of people who are simultaneously a racial minority there are ideological as well as scientific questions to be addressed. The questions he suggests the social-service workers check in their own minds are as follows; (I have substituted the word "Indian" for the word "Negro" in every case).

- Is Indian inequality explainable by external events in society or by internal characteristics of the Indian, his family, his community?
- Is it primarily a problem of the larger white society or of the Indian minority?
- Is it mainly an issue of power or money?
- Is the Indian oppressed or disadvantaged?

- Is he burdened or a burden?
- Must he achieve change in social relationships or only an increment in his own resources?
- Should he look to his strengths and actively influence his own condition, or to his weaknesses and be content to be the passive beneficiary of clever social engineering?
- Is he, finally, a victim of brutal racism, or just another peasant immigrant, but with brown skin?

Audrey Provost, Edmonton

Audrey Provost is a Blackfoot in Edmonton. She laughs and admits that this puts her in a special category. The Blackfoot are a southern Alberta people. When they go to a city it is Calgary or Lethbridge or Medicine Hat. The Indian people in Edmonton are usually Cree or Chipewyan people from the north. Audrey laughs again. "I know that they say that the Blackfoot and the Cree are enemies and that we don't get along," she says. "But that's not always true."

Audrey is twenty-five. Tall, slim, self-possessed. She has long shining black hair parted in the middle and tied in two braids that fall, held by beaded clasps, in front of her shoulders. She has large dark almond-shaped eyes that smile and engage. She is in Edmonton now for the second time. Her first attempt was in the mid-1970s when she came to attend the University of Alberta. That visit lasted eight months. This time she has been in the city for two and a half years and she works for a government-sponsored project helping unemployed native women. Still she talks about going home, sometime, to live.

I'm from a Blackfoot reserve that is in the very south of Alberta just west of Lethbridge about sixty miles. I went to school on the reserve for quite a few years, was bussed to school in the local town for about three years, and then I had the opportunity to go away to school. It was one of Indian Affairs's schemes to get Indians off the reserves and into integrated schools. That was when I was fourteen. My sister and I were going to go to Medicine Hat. We were supposed to go to a public high school there and board with a white family. All we were given was a name on a piece of paper and told to go to the bus depot on a certain evening at a certain time and there would be a bus ticket waiting for us. So we left.

There were quite a few of us; I'd say there was about thirty, thirty-five. All from the Peigan and Blood reserves. We got there quite late at night and there were lots of people around the bus depot because everybody had come to meet somebody so everybody was standing around with a little piece of paper and we had a little piece of paper with the name of the family we were supposed to contact. There was one little lady from Indian Affairs who was supposed to sort it all out. Eventually we found our landlady and landlord and we went home with them and we lived there for a whole year.

It was really kind of scary; really terrifying. It was kind of a shock to wake up on the first morning and realize "I'm really here and now I have to go to this other school across town." It was really scary and you just wanted to pack up and go back home. That was exactly how I felt. At the same time I was glad to be there. I had wanted to go there, to get away from the reserve and that little town.

That first year there must have been seven or eight of us from Brocket. We hung around together all the time; we never let go of each other. It was hard for a lot of the kids. I'll bet not even fifty per cent finished. They were really strict with us. You had to abide by the rules of the house you were in. If you didn't, if there were too many complaints about you, you just had to pack up and leave. The same if you didn't do well in school. A lot of the kids would get really lonesome, they just couldn't cope with it any more. So they would go home. It was hard. But I went back for three years, until I had my grade eleven. Then I went to Lethbridge for my last year.

When I first came to Edmonton, I had a lot of problems that I was leaving behind. I had a little girl that I left behind with my mom and I came to the city by myself. I didn't have any money. I stopped in Calgary overnight with my sister and she gave me enough money for the fare to Edmonton. When I was leaving Calgary I phoned Indian Affairs in Edmonton and I talked to a social worker and told her my situation, how I wanted to come up to Edmonton and go to school. It was in the late fall. That September I had been accepted by the University of Alberta but because of the problems I was having at home I didn't get up here until late. When I got off the bus in Edmonton I only had thirty cents in my hand. But I was determined that I was going to make it for myself.

The social worker had been really nice on the phone. She said that when I got to the city I should come by and she would talk to me and help me. I told her I wanted to bring my little girl to the city too.

Coming into Edmonton I was getting really terrified. I had never seen Edmonton. I just knew it was the capital of Alberta. But coming in there were all these big high-rise buildings as you come off the Calgary Trail. It was really scary. I was really nervous. I was wondering, "what am I going to do?" I didn't even have the address of Indian Affairs, I just had the name of the lady I was supposed to reach.

The bus stopped at the south-side depot and I had this feeling that I should get off because a lot of other people were getting off. But I didn't, I stayed on until the main depot. Then I looked up the address of Indian Affairs in the phone book. There were people all over the place. I just walked around and then I asked a couple of people "how do I get to this address?" They just told me to "catch that bus, catch this bus." So I got on one bus. Luckily thirty cents was what the buses cost then because that was all the money I had left. So I kept getting on different buses and they kept giving me transfers and I was going every which way. It took me all afternoon before I finally got to the Indian Affairs office. I found that it was just half a block away from the south-side bus depot where I was going to get off in the first place. It had taken me all day to get back there. Boy, I was just a bundle of nerves by then.

I went to see the social worker. Luckily I got there just before they closed. But she said that she couldn't help me because I was single and didn't have my little girl with me. She referred me to a halfway house and told me to go there and stay there and try to get a job. She said she would give me enough money for a bus pass, but she gave me a cheque. It was after three already and I had to run all over trying to cash this cheque. It took me the rest of the day to find the halfway house. I was really lost. It was a day I'll never forget.

I stayed at the halfway house for four months. The next day I went out to find a job. I went to the Canada Manpower office. I kept getting lost but I would stop in stores to ask directions and finally I'd walked all the way down to Canada Manpower and I checked out the job bank. There wasn't much but I spent a long hard day walking around trying to find a job. On my way back to the halfway house I passed the Holiday Inn and I thought, "I should apply there for a chambermaid". It wasn't too far from where I was living. So the next morning I went to the Holiday Inn and said that I would like to apply for a job and they hired me as a waitress in their coffee shop. That went really well. I worked there until December, then I went to the university again and applied. They accepted me and I started in January.

I went back home and got my little girl and brought her back up here. But it was so hard. Just trying to pull things together. You know when you're new in the city and you don't know your way around too much. I was given just a little living allowance. I found a day-care centre for my daughter that was just three blocks away. But it was a long three blocks when you have to carry her. And a bag of books. Half of my little allowance was going to this day care when I didn't even know that the place was government subsidized. I could have had it for maybe twenty dollars a month. But nobody told me. You're supposed to ask, I guess, but I didn't even know there was such a thing. I had so many problems. I was poor. And I was so lonely. I met maybe a couple of people but there were no relatives or anybody like that. I spent a lot of money on phone calls. And to top it all off, I'd left my husband but after I was in Edmonton one month I discovered that I was pregnant.

I didn't last out. I withdrew. I stayed eight months and then I went back home. I was there for two and a half years before I came back.

I came back the second time because the man I'm living with now came here to work. That was two and a half years ago. This time I had grown a bit and I knew that when there were things to be done you had to get busy and do them. For instance before we came I resigned from my job back home and I got busy and applied through Native Outreach here for a job in Edmonton. So this time when I came here there was a job waiting for me. I've been at this present job since August '78.

I can relate when some of the girls come in here and tell me how lonely they are because I sat in a little basement suite all through my first winter. We spent a whole winter down there; me sitting and trying to study while all the time in the back of my mind I'm worried about home and missing people and how I've got no social life. You need that for your sanity. And when you have a two-year-old baby that's crawling around and you're expecting another one it can be really heavy on you. And you don't know what all the services are. Sure, they can say "Go look in the Aid Book" [directory] but I didn't even know there was such a thing. All I had was a phone book. That's all I had to look through and find things.

Then you run into people who have problems themselves. Like when I was waitressing at the Holiday Inn, this other waitress, she didn't like me. I know she didn't like me. She always used to call me Pocahontas. I didn't want them to know I was pregnant. But after a while I started to show. But I didn't want to quit because I was making good money with the tips and all. The other waitress used to ask me, "You're pregnant, aren't you; you're going to have a baby. Does the boss know?" She wouldn't get off my back. I used to drink a lot of milk. She always used to say to me; "Audrey, you'd better not drink white milk, you'd better drink chocolate milk. You want to have a chocolate baby, you don't want to have a white baby. What would you do with a white baby?"

That really used to burn me up. I'd have to walk out of there and go fume someplace. I'd cool down then and I'd say to myself; "I have to work, I have to have money. I have to buy furniture. I have a little girl that's coming up here. I can't just walk off the job because somebody doesn't like me and says things to me."

You run into prejudice. I remember when I lived in Lethbridge the year after I graduated from high school, my husband and I were looking for an apartment. I'm telling you we must have combed that city trying to find an apartment. We found one at a place where the caretakers were friends of ours. We looked at it and we really liked it. So we put down a damage deposit. There was a big sign out in front of the building that there was a one-bedroom apartment for rent. It was a small place, but nice. We were really looking for a place because we had been driving every day between the reserve and the college. But somehow the owner found our phone number in Brocket and phoned us. He said, "I hear you're going to move in on the first." Then he says that he'd like to meet us and he gives us his address and asks us to come to his place. So we went and it was a nice big house. And he just wanted to look at us. Then, the next day he phoned us and said; "Could you go back over to the caretaker and pick up your money because it was a mistake, that place was already taken." So we went over and picked up our money. And for about two months we drove by that place and there was still a big sign out front "For Rent".

When we came to Edmonton we had a hard time finding a place. Finally I just started asking, "Do you rent to Indians?" I phoned one man and he said that he had a place for rent. So I asked him if I could come and look at it and he said "sure". So we went there but he wouldn't even open the door. He just peeked out a little bit and then he put his chain on and locked it. He said, "I'm sorry, it's taken." And I said "Well I just phoned a little while ago." He said "I know, but it's taken." So we got in the car and we drove half a block, just half a block, and I phoned back that same number and asked if he had an apartment for rent and he said "yes". And I said to him, "Do you rent to Indians?" And he said "No, because there was a lady here just now that gave me a rough time." I gave him no rough time. I said to him, "I'm that lady." I said, "Would you like it if the human rights called you up?" Then he started stuttering away about how he liked all kinds of people. I never called the Human Rights Commission.

My cousin went to human rights once and he got a public apology. He had gone into a drug store and he wanted to buy a bottle of rubbing alcohol. But the druggist said "No, I don't sell it to Indians because they drink it and they go crazy." So my cousin walked outside and got his wife who is white to go in and she bought it. Then they both went in and they went to the Human Rights Commission.

I think for anyone who leaves the reserve to live in the city it's such a big adjustment to make. I used to get headaches all the time; from the rushing, the noise, the traffic, the pollution. All that was just dragging me down. Pretty soon you're just racing. Whereas on the reserve everything is so quiet, your days are long. Here it's red light, green light, yellow light; everything just goes, goes, goes. I've learned to cope with it. I just close the curtains, listen to music, and enjoy my kids. I know my way around now. There isn't anything if I want to do it that I can't. Swimming, skating; if I want to take my kids to the museum or if I just want to drive around the city I'm able to do it now, where before I was scared and I just stayed in one place.

Being status still applies for some benefits when I am in the city: I can get free medical or things like glasses and so on through Indian Affairs. And my daughter's education is paid for, her school supplies and so on.

I want to stay in the city for a few years, but I'd like to move back to the reserve sometime. I'd like to work with my own people. I see that there's a lot of potential there. Especially with the knowledge I've gained working here. Plus there's the cost of living. I could get a house down there. It's really expensive living here.

Also I'd like to have my kids back there and have them go to school with Indian kids. Here they're involved with Indian dancing, but they always look forward to going home. My oldest girl wants to go back. She's only seven, but she's always saying "when are we going to go back?" I'd like to have them get to know their relatives. Our family on the reserve is really close. People there meet us and with my daughter, they take her hand and they say "I'm your auntie or I'm your cousin." She really likes that, she wants to know them.

The Inevitable Urban Indian

In the early 1960s Cyril Keeper, a young non-status Indian, moved with his family from Berens River, high on the east side of Lake Winnipeg, to the city of Winnipeg. Keeper's father had been a fisherman. But when the bottom fell out of the freshwater fish market he felt obliged to pack up his family, including young Cyril, and move south to the city. In 1980, Cyril Keeper, by now thirty-six, was elected to the House of Commons from a downtown Winnipeg constituency.

Though Cyril Keeper may be seen as an exceptional person, his story is not exceptional. One by one, more and more Indian people are taking their places in seats of action and influence in the city. Keeper, before his election to Parliament, was both an academic and a member of Winnipeg's city council. His career is mirrored by that of a growing and interesting collection of artists, professionals, teachers, social workers, tradespeople, bureaucrats. In 1978 a national Indian lawyers' association was launched in Calgary and it immediately claimed a couple of dozen native lawyers and students. These are people who a decade ago were little in evidence; now they are increasingly visible and their numbers, sophistication, and influence continue to grow.

The urbanization of Indian and Métis people in Canada is inevitable. They are joining a movement of millions of rural peoples around the world; a movement that has been swelling during most of this century. The native people now living in large numbers in Winnipeg and Edmonton, in Regina,

Vancouver, Calgary, Toronto, Saskatoon, and Montreal are not some political refugees waiting for a chance to return to their homelands; despite the periodic longings toward the reserves and the frequent pull of the rural communities, they are essentially in the cities to stay. High reserve birth rates, limited reserve economies, the attraction of the bright city lights force the migration and make it a matter of historical course.

Native people in the cities fall into two groups. There is the large group of newly-arrived people who are most visible and who, with the combination of difficulty with language, lack of money, few (or no) industrial skills, lack of urban sophistication and the racial prejudice of the large community, endure a treacherous day-to-day existence trying to feed, clothe, and house themselves.

But there is the second group, people like Cyril Keeper; better educated, sophisticated persons who have been in the cities for some time and know the levers. They are people who have succeeded with life's economic necessities and are ready to use the excess energy to carve a distinctive place for themselves in the community.

Both groups are growing. The second group continues to grow with the graduates of the first group. The first group grows as more people come in to the city and join those who fail to graduate and slip instead into the maelstrom, condemned for generations to be the urban poor. Both groups continue to be impatient in their own ways; the first with its poverty and hard life, the second with the frustrations of getting a toe-hold in the power structure of the urban community.

But both groups are in the city as native people. Fewer and fewer Indian people in the cities are slinking around pretending they are Chinese or wanting to believe they are Mexicans. Indian people are increasingly determined to resist what has to this point been called assimilation; the impulse to become "brown white men". Many more people all the time feel free to identify themselves as native and do it with authority.

So much so is this occurring that anthropologists and sociologists are beginning to talk about a new ethnicity; the urban Indian. The urban Indian is identified not by his reserve affiliation or by his treaty status or by his socio-economic position. He or she is identified by ethnicity and heritage and by the fact of having made a conscious choice to maintain and reinforce that ethnicity and heritage, even (or especially) while living in the city. One Indian leader in Regina compared his people to the Jews, whose identity is forged by a combination of adherence to traditional values and a history of being outcasts from the larger society. In his mind those same elements would be the ones to create and strengthen the native identity in the city. Similarly, the native organizations, clubs, social centres, churches, that have sprung up in the cities should not be seen, he felt, as temporary institutions meant simply to smooth the transition from reserve or rural area to city, but as the beginnings of a growing infrastructure for an Indian urban culture.

The life of Indian people in Canada for the past two centuries has been one of enormous heartache and struggle. The move to the cities is a part of that struggle. It may or may not be the culmination of the struggle. It is too early to tell. The fact that it is a period of problems and disruptions for both the Indian people and the cities will continue to be demonstrated vividly for the next decade and perhaps beyond that. The urban issues discussed in this book, the places where Indian people and the urban communities reach frustrations or conflict will remain issues for the foreseeable future. The flux between the two groups of Indian people will continue.

There will be anxieties and much gnashing of teeth about the ways in which whites and Indians, mainstream urban organizations and Indian organizations relate; whether purposes are to master one another, compete with one another, or help support one another. There will be no easy answers. But both the cities and the Indians will know one thing; the native people are not in the cities as guests or as tourists. The cities, too, are part of their birthright. As the reserves and the land once was theirs, so will the cities be theirs. Their growing presence will very much decide the shape of those cities.